Kilim
History and Symbols

DARIO VALCARENGHI

KILIM
HISTORY AND
SYMBOLS

Electa / Abbeville
Milan   New York

Translation
Huw Evans

Front Cover
Kilim "of the two red
goddesses" (cat. 124)

The publication of the
original Italian edition
of this volume was made
possible also thanks to
the contributions of the
MAT—Museo per le
Arti Tessili—and the
Fondazione Sartirana
Arte, as well as Imprefin
SIM, Cassa di Risparmio
di Roma Group

ISBN 1-55859-880-4

© 1994 by **Electa**, Milan
Elemond Editori Associati

First U.S. edition

Contents

The Anatolian Kilim and Its Symbolic Meaning

The Anatolian kilim is the expression of a tradition dating back around nine thousand years: a tradition that has been maintained by women without a break for hundreds of generations and almost up to our own day, as we shall see. The technique has been handed down from mother to daughter over the centuries and throughout recorded history.

It is a mysterious tradition, of which much remains to be deciphered, since it requires the interpretation of symbols, and the understanding of their deeper meaning presupposes a program of research that covers the entire history of humanity, taking in aspects of philosophy, religion, alchemy, and psychoanalysis. A highly complex task, therefore, that few people are in a position to undertake.

The signs and symbols have hidden meanings, often unknown even to those who make and create them, and thus communicate feelings and values without the intervention of the conscious mind.

For centuries and millennia, then, the women of Anatolia have woven designs that have always been the same, geometric patterns and stylized figures, passing them down in silence and without any perception of them as representing a female culture.

In the Neolithic era, that is in the infancy of the human race, when the kilim was born, the images surfaced spontaneously from the inner world, speaking of its eternal protagonists: love, life, death, and power. Thus it is possible to trace in the unchanging decorative forms of the kilim a means of communication that was developed by cultures remote in time, and that can explain to us insights, thoughts, and feelings through records that are several thousand years older than writing itself.

It is the aim of this book to try to find out some of the meanings that were at-tached to kilims long ago, accepting the cultural challenge that is concealed behind the silent enigma of those shapes and colors. *Kilim* in Turkish means "woven material," in this case a rough and protective textile that is warm and, at the same time, cool, brightly colored and durable. This is what the kilim must have been in the life of the ancient peoples of Asia Minor, whether nomadic or settled.

That rug was a friendly presence: it provided shelter from the wind and the sand, served as a table or a bed; it functioned as a social space for discussions and chatter; as a cradle for babies, a funeral pall, a container for objects, a place for prayer. In the most ancient civilizations, as we shall see later on, no distinction was made between objects of everyday use and those used for religious purposes, and kilims, which were also employed for both functions and generally formed part of a bride's dowry, were woven by women.[1]

The connection between kilims and women's work does not depend solely on sociological and historical factors, but also on symbolic and religious ties. The kilim, which is not just a utilitarian object but also a symbolic one, appears to be closely intertwined with the archetypal universe of the feminine principle. As the archeologist Marija Gimbutas has clearly indicated with reference to the culture of the kurgans (middle-eastern Russia): "[...] the old European sacred images and symbols were never totally uprooted; these most persistent features in human history were too deeply implanted in the psyche. They could have disappeared only with the total extermination of the female population [...]. The old European culture was the matrix of much later beliefs and practices. Memories of a long-lasting gynocentric past could not be erased, and it is not surprising that the feminine principle plays a formidable role in the subconscious dream and fantasy world. It remains (in Jungian terminology) 'the repository of human experience' and a 'depth structure.' To an archeologist it is an extensively documented historical reality."[2]

In fact all the scholars who have studied weaving are in agreement on tracing its origin back to the female world,[3] owing to the numerous symbolic connections that we shall be looking at further on, but primarily and chiefly because it has been seen as an image of creation, a birth that comes out of the union of two opposites (the warp and the weft).

"The work of weaving is a work of creation, a birth. When the textile is finished, the weaver cuts the threads that link it to the loom and, while doing this, pronounces a formula of blessing that is the same as the one used by the midwife when she severs the umbilical cord of a newborn child. Everything takes place as if weaving were the translation of a mysterious human anatomy into a simple language."[4]

The connection between weaving and the world of women is supported, in the writings of Bachofen, by a huge range of sources: "Twisting the thread is a symbolic action that crops up fairly often and is founded on the same conception to which is linked the act of spinning or weaving typical of the great mother nature. Thus we see Aphrodite weaving, as well as Penelope, Circe and Maia Persephone, the three *anus textrices* (old weavers) of the underworld, who carry out their work without lifting their gaze; again in the act of weaving we find the Fates, Tanaquil, Gaia, Caecilia, Eileihyia, the priestesses of Diana, and the Syrian goddess Aphrodite Urania at Athens, whom for this reason is represented with a spindle. The goddess of Sais is also the inventor and patron of weaving, and the veil that covers her has the same significance as that of Helen, Vesta and the Grace—which is why the latter is said to be finely veiled in the *Iliad*—and of the golden Χερό-

μακτρον (cloth) that Demeter gives to Rampsintos when he visits her in the underworld. It also has the same meaning as the *laciniae* (cloths) that were offered to Ceres as votive gifts in Apuleius; as the ribbons that are associated chiefly with Ceres and in the cult of the dead are placed in a privileged relationship with the chthonic forces. Weaving is an attribute that the divinity also passes on to her priestesses. In the preparation of the great and splendid dress that the Athenians wove for Pallas Athene, the matrons of Elea for Juno, and the women of Amyclae for Apollo, a sacred act is carried out that corresponds to the very nature of the divinity and is intended to imitate it. This is the reason why weaving is so often connected with worship of the great maternal divinities: with the Aphrodite of Kos [...], with the cult of Isis [...], with the cult of the γυνή επιχωρία [woman of the place] of Patrae [...]. The Lydian Arachne has the same meaning [...], the net of Diana Dictynna has the same meaning [...] as does the net with which the Delphic omphalos and other, similar divine stones were covered [...]."[5]

The principal phases in the production of the kilim were spinning, dyeing and weaving. So it is worth taking a look at these last two operations and the connections that existed in antiquity between their technological and ritual aspects, and therefore between the product and its significance.

As is well known, color has represented a magical and religious means of expression of fundamental importance since the most ancient of times. The oldest surviving records of the use of color date from a hundred thousand years ago, from the first burials in which the human remains were piled up in a space bounded by a red circle traced on the ground.[6] In the cave paintings at Altamira (Spain) and Lascaux (France), dating from fifteen thousand years ago, the religious and

magical use of color is evident.

In this connection Mircea Eliade has written: "In the Paleolithic period there is evidence for the use more or less everywhere of red ocher, a ritual substitute for blood, symbols of life, as a testimony to the belief in an existence after death [...]. Recent archeological discoveries have shown that hematite was mined [...] forty-three thousand years ago [...]. Among the various examples: the burial place at Chapelle aux Saints, in the Corrèze, where the grave contained the body and numerous flint and iron tools painted with red ocher. In the excavations of Tell Ramab (Syria), where skullcaps have been found with the forehead painted red and the face modeled in plaster [...], the bodies sprinkled with red ocher were laid to rest in the graves with shells, charms and necklaces; the burials were oriented toward the east revealing the intention of linking the fate of the soul with the course of the sun."[7] Ever since that time and right down to the present day, color has maintained a particularly strong symbolic value, and for convergent reasons has been studied by historians of religion, alchemists, and depth psychologists. Through color it was possible to convey messages, ideas, and emotions. Even today passion, hope, pain, and purity remain analogically linked to different colors, and yet much of the profundity and complexity of the language has been lost. After all the universal character—and not just in a geographical sense, but also in a cosmological and psychological one—of the symbolism of colors should come as no surprise if we just try for a moment to imagine the ecstatic wonder and magical rapture of the first human beings to *have become aware* of color: red was not red, but the poppy, fire, the sunset. Where did red come from? How could it be made when it was needed? The human beings who, little by little, over the course of time, succeeded in reproducing first one color and then another, must have thought that they were drawing near to the divinity and challenging its monopoly of creation, since to color something was to imitate what the great nature goddess had done.

Hence it is comprehensible that a religious and therefore symbolic character should have been attributed to this operation right from the start, and that each color (depending on the time and culture) should have assumed a particular significance.

The mythical attribution of a discovery or invention to a god (as in the story of Prometheus and fire) attests to the sacred value attached to the feat. In legend dyeing, as F. Brunello reminds us, is a divine invention: "The god Merkart, walking along the beach with his dog, noticed that the animal's muzzle had taken on a red color. Intrigued, the god discovered that the color came from certain shellfish washed up on the beach that the dog had been sniffing. Then the god Merkart, desiring to do something pleasing to his lover, the nymph Tyros, decided to give her a tunic dyed by his own hand with the bright color of the murices, thus becoming the first to use purple dye."[8]

Thus finding and getting to know the dye and the way it worked, learning how to transfer it onto cloth, as onto other materials, was in remote antiquity an initiatory knowledge, a sacred activity handed down, according to precise rules and instructions, from generation to generation. And so—just as with other bodies of ritual knowledge—the art of dyeing in the Neolithic period (and even in more recent times) assigned a special power to those who practiced it: the power of those who know *how it is done*, but above all the power of those who know *what it means*.

In this connection, a number of documents exist that refer to the suspicion and anxiety aroused, in the distant past, by the art of dyeing, insofar as it was considered the manifestation of an occult power.

Dyeing, for instance, scared the Dorians who had occupied the Peloponnese, subjugating the Mycenean peoples. According to tradition, they even went so far as to forbid dyers from living in cities and decreed that wool clothing should remain in the crude state. Little by little, however, the custom of dying fabrics got the better of the conquerors' fear, and the Peloponnesians went back to brightening up their clothes, textiles and footwear with red dye.[9]

How did the women of Anatolia, in ancient times, dye their kilims? Naturally we have no information on the matter as far as the Neolithic period of Çatal Hüyük is concerned, but we do know that, in the following period and right up to the end of the last century (when chemically synthesized dyes had already been imported for almost fifty years), the dye was natural, which means of mineral, animal and vegetable origin.

From stones, shells, herbs, flowers, shellfish, insects, roots and seaweed, powders of different tones and shades were extracted. These were then transferred onto the wool and *fixed* by means of special technical procedures that have now been completely lost to us.

In the second part of this book, I shall set out to explain my views on the symbology of color in kilims. In these pages, however, I shall confine myself to pointing out that it was not so much a question of stylistic, formal or aesthetic needs, but of symbolic meanings.

Weaving, the final phase in the manufacture of the kilim, was what gave meaning to the whole of the work. Apart from the color and apart from the significance of every design, what was the symbolic value of weaving in itself? Why did the ancients attribute this activity to the gods?

Weaving involves crossing two threads, the warp and the weft, one vertical and the other horizontal, one stretched taut and the other undulating and intertwined with the first. To produce the textile it is necessary for these two threads to be bound, otherwise each will remain a fragile and fluttering potentiality. There is hardly any need to point out that the awareness of the need for these two opposites to meet raised profound echoes in the human mind, evoking analogies of various kinds.

If the meeting of opposites does not take place, nothing is created, for each element is defined by its opposite and takes its meaning from it.

As the physicist and philosopher of science Fritjof Capra has written: "Solely by the act of concentrating our attention on any concept, we create its opposite."[10]

No energy is created without bipolarity, without positive and negative. No child is born without the meeting of a man and a woman. Good without evil, dark without light, death without life remain abstract virtualities. Whatever contains opposites (in this case the loom) refers to the whole and therefore to the cosmos, to a universal dimension that, in ancient times, was identified with the image of nature that included every element and its opposite, and therefore with that of the Mother Goddess who embodied it. This is why Bachofen is able to say succinctly: "The image of spinning and weaving represents the activity of the creative and shaping force of nature. The activity of the great originary mother of matter is compared with skillful twisting and weaving, which gives articulation, symmetrical form and delicacy to the raw material."[11]

In indirect confirmation of all this, a number of accounts dating from not very many years ago relate that in the more isolated villages of North Africa "[...] the vertical axis of the loom is called *axis of the sky* and the horizontal one *axis of the earth*. These [...] pieces of wood already symbolize the whole universe."[12]

If the loom and what was produced on it were, long ago, symbols of the whole, it is understandable why, in more recent times, they have assumed a significance connected with destiny.

The idea of destiny is contained in the space between life and death. For the ancients, it was destiny to be born, destiny to die, and what lay in the middle, shrouded in mystery, was contained between these two extremes. This is why the cloth, the loom, the thread and the spindle have so often been associated with the image of fate.

Many are the goddesses represented with spindles, looms and shuttles in their hands, who preside, as images of all-embracing nature, over the passing of time and the succession of events. Some of these divinities, including the great Hittite goddess depicted in statuettes dating from 2000 BC and that have survived to the present day, decided the life span of mortals. At times they took on the aspect of beneficent creativity, at others that of terrible destruction, always incarnating the harsh and pitiless law of necessity, the law that required the incessant changing of beings and the endless variety of manifestations.

In this context it is impossible not to be reminded of the Fates of Greek tradition. The first spins the thread of life and its events, the second measures the length on the basis of unfathomable calculations, and the third cuts the thread, bringing death. Between the beginning and the end of this work existence unfolds in a cycle of eternal recurrence, ruled by the supreme natural law of transformation.

In the Helladic era even the Olympian gods were subject to this law, a mark of the power of the great goddess nature that had survived the establishment of a patriarchal culture. Not so from the Middle Ages onward in the West. How is it that, since the fourteenth century, such words as "warp" and "web"[13] have acquired a hostile and negative value? Ever since that time the sacred coordinates of the loom have also been used to describe subterranean and silent acts and secret intrigues, for over the course of time the disparagement of female culture has produced a whole range of consequences for language as well, including—as far as the purposes of this book are concerned—the language of weaving, as a traditional activity of women.

In the cultural context of the fourteenth century the majestic force and inductive and analogical wisdom of the feminine principle were demonized by a patriarchal culture that, in the first place, was afraid of them and that was no longer capable of accepting the complexity of the female universe with its insidious and alarming areas of darkness, but also with its profound and illuminating intuitions.

The consequent *policy*, which was to reduce the power of women to the level of machination and plotting, justified its repression.

By this time the female world had been split into two: on one side the women absorbed into male culture, on the other the rebels who had formed a pact with the devil, resorting to black magic, practicing witchcraft and human sacrifice at their sabbaths.

The witch hunt marked the formal beginning of this split that was not only to cost millions of lives, but also to have dramatic, and perhaps incalculable, consequences for the subsequent history of Western civilization, which has remained, right down to the present day, bereft of the polarity of female knowledge and understanding.

From time immemorial, in symbolic terms, Athene has been dead in our culture and only Hecate has survived.[14]

The web is no longer that of Penelope, preserving life and love, but that of a black spider weaving death.

René Guénon has made some interesting comments on the symbolism of weaving, in the sense that I am proposing. The writer has put forward the hypothesis that every intersection of a thread of the warp with a thread of the weft traces a cross, and that each interlacing of the textile constitutes its center. The cross, as is well known, is a symbol of totality in which, according to Guénon, the horizontal axis is the human axis and the vertical axis is what transcends it. The "symbolism of weaving [...] is also employed to represent the world, or more exactly the set of all the worlds, that is the set of states or degrees that, in undefined multitude, constitutes universal Existence [...]. From another point of view it can be said that the manifestation of a being in a certain state of existence, like the occurrence of any event, is determined by the meeting of a thread of the warp with a thread of the weft. Thus each thread of the warp is a being considered in its essential nature that, as a direct projection of the principal *Self*, constitutes the *link among all its states* maintaining its own unity through their indeterminate multiplicity."[15]

A consideration of the significance of the language of weaving leads to another series of reflections, which I shall investigate further at a later stage, connected with the hypothesis that weaving was, in its origins, a form of symbolic writing, in which the unconscious need to unite opposites in a dual totality became the object of a *handed-down sign*.

I believe, in conclusion, that it is possible to see the Anatolian kilim as the oldest textile known to us, used in the family, social and religious life of the peoples of Asia Minor, and consider it the product—perhaps the most significant one—of a female tradition that has passed it on substantially unchanged down to our own day.

In dyeing and in weaving, in the entire *tekné* of the kilim, the women of Anatolia were not so much looking to achieve aesthetic and formal results as expressing the sense, keen even though unconscious, of a symbolic culture of Anatolian origin.

On the basis of the foregoing considerations, the differences between the kilim and the knotted rug[16] are not confined to differences of technology, but also entail a diversity of origin and meaning.

In this sense I feel that the intuitions of J. Thompson and B. Balpinar are justified, but do not go far enough.[17] It is common knowledge that the knotted rug, like the kilim, is woven on a loom, but that tiny knots with threads of different colors are tied on the interlacing of warp and weft so as to form a particular pattern. The knots (of which there can be as many as a million per square meter) permit the creation of a very complex design, something that it is obviously impossible to obtain with the kilim. The knotting, finally, introduces a third element into the original duality of the two directions of the kilim. This operation may have a symbolic value, for while two is the number representing opposites, in that it contains within itself the one and the other, three is the number of the synthesis that establishes a new point of departure, laying the foundations for the creation of a new opposite. From this point of view two is a *feminine receptive* number and three is a *masculine penetrative* number, since the former embraces a totality and the latter prepares a new opposition.

Following this symbolic line of thought, we may be able to understand more clearly why the kilim, unlike the knotted rug, was woven exclusively by women. The art of weaving the kilim was transmitted orally from mother to daughter in keeping with a symbolic tradition that was unconscious but powerful and active.

The knotted rug, on the other hand, was almost always made on the basis of a drawn *pattern* and thus of a fixed scheme to be copied. It is therefore understandable why, over the course of time, colors, forms and designs should have changed, in step with changes in society and culture: in the unconscious of the weaver the symbolic dimension of the signs was not so strong as to make tradition prevail over aesthetic and formal research and over the fascination of the new.

[1] In this connection cf. too K.R. Veenhot, *Aspects of Old Assyrian Trade and Its Terminology*, Leiden 1972, p. 90; "[...] it is evident from pre-Islamic medieval sources that the weavers were women, whether they worked independently or supervised the work of other weavers. This is quite clear from the tablets written by Assyrian and Hittite women. The weavers, who lived in towns and cities, or their neighborhood, were usually the wives of merchants and some of them also belonged to the priestly class."

[2] M. Gimbutas, *The Language of the Goddess*, Thames and Hudson, London 1989, pp. 316-320.

[3] Cf., among others, the writings of R. Guénon, J. Servier and J. J. Bachofen. The only exception to this is found in ancient Egypt where, it appears, men were weavers as well.

[4] Var. Authors, *Dictionnaire des symboles*, Seghers, Paris 1980, vol. IV, p. 300. These words refer to a still living tradition in the mountain villages of North Africa.

[5] J. J. Bachofen, *Il simbolismo funerario degli antichi*, Italian edition, Guida, Naples 1989, pp. 523, 524. (Original title: *Versuch Über die Gräbersymbolic der Alten*).

[6] A. Leroi-Gourhan, *I popoli senza scrittura*, Italian edition, Laterza, Bari 1978, pp. 8,9. (Original title: *Histoirie des Religions*).

[7] M. Eliade, *Storia delle credenze e delle idee religiose*, Sansoni, Florence 1980.

[8] F. Brunello, *L'arte della tintura nella storia dell'umanità*, Neri-Pozzi, Vicenza 1968.

[9] The concept is taken from Sabatino Moscati, *I Fenici*, UTET, Turin 1972.

[10] F. Capra, *Il Tao della Fisica*, Italian edition, Adelphi, Milan, 1982, p. 165. (Original title: *The Tao of Physics*).

[11] J. J. Bachofen, op. cit., p. 525.

[12] Var. Authors, op. cit., vol. IV, p. 300.

[13] Cf. *The Chambers Dictionary*, Chambers Harrap, London 1993, pp. 1963, 1976.

[14] Hecate was a goddess of the night, the moon, and the underworld, dangerous to man and favorably disposed toward women. Cruel and bloodthirsty, she was a shadow image of the original Mother Goddess that had survived in Greek culture.

[15] R. Guénon, *Il simbolismo della croce*, Italian edition, Rusconi, Milan 1973, p. 115. (Original title: *Le Symbolisme de la Croix*).

[16] Characterized by its pile (knot).

[17] "The main stream of kilim weaving is an old, independent and autonomous tradition owing little to pile weaving or embroidery," J. Thompson, *The Undiscovered Kilim*, David Black, London 1977, p. 19.

"Among all these different types of weaving kilims must be the oldest and so it is through them that ancient symbols and designs have passed to other rugs," B. Balpinar, *The Goddess from Anatolia*, Eskenazi, Milan 1989, vol. IV, p. 1.

Myths and History of the Anatolian Kilim

To the best of our knowledge, where did the kilim originate and when? The trail comes to a stop at Çatal Hüyük (Neolithic pottery, *circa* 7000 BC), the oldest settlement ever to have been discovered thanks to the ingenious work of the British archeologist J. Mellaart. Çatal Hüyük is located in Turkey, in the Anatolian region, to the southeast of the modern city of Konya.

So far fourteen levels have been brought to light, covering an area of thirty-two hectares, but the zone that has been excavated is equivalent to about three per cent of the town as a whole.[1]

It is reckoned that there were at least a thousand houses for a population that was not less than six thousand (possibly with several thousand in neighboring villages).

Since the seventh millennium BC, this town had made its living from farming and stock raising. Later it began to produce and trade pottery, wooden vessels, baskets, mats, figured textiles and tools made from copper, lead, and obsidian (a volcanic rock that was used instead of iron).

Thus it was a complex settlement comparable for at least three reasons, according to James Mellaart, to the cultures of three thousand years later, the ones of the so-called recent phases of the fourth millennium. Initially it developed in the manner of a hive, without roads to separate the buildings: the constructions are built back-to-back and communicating with one another (fig. 1). In addition, no written documents have been found at Çatal Hüyük, and there are no traces of monumental buildings. Later on we shall see how these three characteristics are a decisive factor in assigning the civilization to the culture of the mother earth.

"Nine thousand years ago," writes James Mellaart, "the visitor to Çatal Hüyük was faced with a series of walls without a break, a sort of rabbit warren made up of two-story houses, with a flat roof and no doors, that could only be entered by means of a ladder that descended from the roof [...]. There were no houses of the type familiar to us. Each house was made up of a rectangular room, with an area of about twenty-five square meters, with the addition of a narrow storeroom on one of the sides; [...] there were no party walls; each house had its own walls and many houses were combined in large blocks, one alongside the other [...]. The blocks of houses were separated by courtyards, which served as areas for the accumulation of household rubbish and for open-air activities. The town had no walls or special fortifications; the external part of the settlement was formed by an unbroken wall without entrance gates, and pens for animals were attached to it."[9]

Mellaart's words describe for us a town without fortifications or walls, but at the same time self-enclosed, protected, and to some extent *round*. The shape of this town is a maternal one resembling, as was pointed out above, a hive, a structure that grew outward in a circle, without any roads (such as the *cardo*

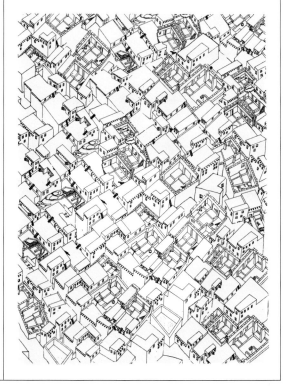

1. Çatal Hüyük. Houses uncovered by the archeological excavations and reconstruction of the part not excavated. The town was inhabited by about six thousand people.

and *decumanus*) to act as axes of development for the settlement.

The absence or primitive character of writing are also typical features of a culture built around the Mother Goddess. In this type of civilization, in fact, it is not as important to organize thought in a systematic manner (as happens with the written word) as to convey it in a symbolic and analogical form connected with the image and with oral communication.

Even in Crete and Mycenae, for example (whose cultures flourished about three thousand years after Çatal Hüyük), written documents did not play a major rule, being used solely to record lists of taxes, goods and duties. What really mattered was handed down orally or through wall paintings, music and religious rites.

Finally the absence of monumental architecture also suggests a world in which the divinity was the Great Goddess, nature, mother earth, the beneficent and terrible primordial energy immanent in the life of all human beings and uncontested mistress of every aspect of existence. So it is possible to understand how worship of the divinity found expression not so much in monumental temples as in domestic constructions, linked with the rhythms of daily life, in close contact with the home, the hearth and animals. The temple, in fact, was a simple room, adjoining the others and just like them. The constructions used for worship were distinguished from ordinary houses by their decoration of a religious character and by the presence of statues and statuettes and of richer graves containing ritual weapons: *it seems that each of them* had been the place of worship for three or four of the surrounding houses.[3]

The presence of the cult of the Mother Goddess, and more generally of the culture connected with it, in the Neolithic period has long raised the question of whether matriarchy existed at the time, something that has still not been settled in scientific circles.

It is my own view that the combined results of research carried out in a variety of disciplines (archeology, anthropology, history of religions, and depth psychology) tend today to make scientists lean toward the hypothesis that a matriarchal phase did in fact exist. Until documentary evidence of this emerges, however, we are obliged to remain at the level of conjecture.

If we consider, moreover, that matriarchy relates to a phase preceding the invention of writing, the obstacles to the discovery of incontrovertible proof of its existence may be insurmountable. As far as the aims of this work are concerned, however, the answer to this question is essentially irrelevant. Matriarchy which, as is well known, signifies *government by the mother*, defines a hypothetical historical era distinguished by the fact that the *law of the mother*, rather than the *law of the father*, held sway in sociopolitical organization and in legal and economic systems. But the symbols of the world of religion and worship lie to some extent outside such areas, which therefore do not affect the origins of the kilim. In other words, in the Neolithic society of the Middle East, men and women, quite apart from the question of which of them were its rulers, were under the influence of the feminine principle on the cultural and religious plane. And it is in the ambit of the culture of the Great Mother, out of which emerged other nameless towns like Çatal Hüyük,[4] that we find the first traces of kilims.

As James Mellaart has pointed out, Çatal Hüyük represents the oldest cradle of civilization known to us, the most ancient site at which the fundamental functions of an organized town life were established. It is here that we find all sorts of objects being used for the first time in the world: the first mirrors, the first pots, the first textiles, the first wooden containers, the first paintings on plastered walls.[5]

And the first kilims too. The excavations have brought to light not only pieces of carbonized fabric, but also fragments of kilims painted on the walls of the houses. In a few cases the frescoes found so far depict naturalistic scenes, such as the eruption of a volcano or scenes from the hunt and daily life, but the majority of them represent geometric and stylized forms that are similar, and often identical, to kilims of the historical, modern and contemporary eras.

In this connection Mellaart has written that the kilims are "easily recognizable by their complicated geometric ornamentation, sewn borders and many colors" and that "two of the wall paintings of sanctuary VII, 21 (6600 BC) at Çatal Hüyük imitate a sewn border. This would make no sense for a painting unless a kilim had been used as a model"[6] (fig. 2).

Faced with the striking similarities among different images (figs. 3, 4, 5, 6 and 7), the researcher is forced to admit the existence of a language that has used the same signs and the same threads to convey its deep truths for about nine thousand years: today this language demands to be deciphered. Why those geometric signs, those abstract and stylized forms that have not changed over the course of time? Is there a code hidden in those symbols and those shapes? What do they mean? As I had occasion to write some years ago[7] and as other authors have observed,[8] the language of kilims is a symbolic language. Yet for this statement not to remain an abstract and in the end sterile proposition, it is necessary to make clear that the signs of that language are evocative of ideas, convictions and states of mind that were deeply rooted in the collective unconscious of the women who wove them. They are symbols of general ideas, of thoughts that were not rationally expressed, but emotionally "felt and shared." The repetition of a series of *typical* signs and equally *typical* interlacings of different forms is reminiscent of what Jung defined as *archetypes* of the collective unconscious, that is *guiding images that are always the same* or even *always identical images of a beginning* in the sense of *arché*; and therefore, when all is said and done, images that are the bearers of a truth that is general and that may be considered eternal. Archetypes are not perceived by the logical and rational part of the human mind, but by the inductive and analogical one, for they do not explain but suggest, do not describe but represent, do not inspire reason but reflection, do not lead to the separation, but to the unification and connection of thoughts.

Just as a woman brings a baby into the world, just as the earth brings forth its fruits, the human being produces an idea that, separating itself from its author, takes on a life of its own. Sticking to this example, the stylized female figure that holds a small shape between its open legs suggests the image, at one and the same time general and archetypal, concrete and abstract, of creativity in natural and intellectual life. In other words: a child can be seen, a flower can be seen, but an idea cannot be seen and has to find a way of being represented before it becomes a written word. At a certain point of evolution this idea entered *thought* and gradually assumed, through successive sedimentations, a form analogical to a phenomenon of nature, perhaps even before it found expression in spoken words and certainly before it did so in written characters. The stylization of *that* natural phenomenon, having become the archetypal image of *that* idea, has remained in the subconscious of humanity, from which it still surfaces today, in the drawings of children, for instance,

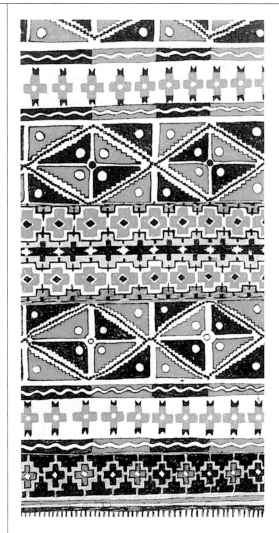

2. *Çatal Hüyük.*
Reconstruction of wall
painting imitating a woven
fabric with fringes.

in dreams or in the patterns of an old kilim. *By its very nature* the archetypal image is steeped in the subconscious. In the Middle Ages and the Renaissance in Europe, philosophers and alchemists rediscovered a symbolic and initiatory language that in ancient times had been the exclusive prerogative of the priestly castes or, at least, of cultured minorities. In more recent times the discovery of the collective unconscious has restored scientific relevance and dignity to this type of investigation, which is still in its infancy.

By now it is easy to understand how the whole of Neolithic culture and many of the successive cultures were founded on a form of communication based on images. During the phase of history in which the human consciousness emerged from the depths of the unconscious, the first general ideas and their connections found spontaneous expression in figures that had assumed a collective value and, as such, were handed down.

They were sacred ideas, and therefore images, because they were representative of a truth uncovered little by little, with great effort, during the awakening of the awareness and the intelligence that the human being has always regarded as sparks of the divine.

For these reasons, it is my belief that in the most ancient civilizations all aspects of consciousness had a religious and initiatory character. The life of the family and the group, at worship and at work, was regulated by ritual laws and imbued with a magically perceived sense of the divine. Faith and daily existence, as I pointed out earlier, did not become separate until later eras. This is why kilims, like everything else, were part of the bride's dowry, objects of everyday use and, at the same time, ritual points of reference connected with religious observances, and why their designs expressed the archetypal ideas of human thought. But, over the course of time, with the subsequent development of individual consciousness and the faculties of logic and reason, the archetypal language has progressively lost its vigor, giving way to mechanisms of personal thinking and to more complex linguistic processes.

The collective *great images*, always at work in the unconscious of humanity, reemerge, for instance, in certain emblematic and apparently meaningless gestures, in dreams and in paintings by young children—i.e. in manifestations of the unconscious—but they are no longer, generally speaking, current in communication between human beings. This is not true as far as kilims are concerned. We are faced, in this case, with one of those extremely rare situations in which the archetypal language has mysteriously survived nine thousand years of human history, remaining true to itself. This is an undoubted fact, since the same decorative themes that were used in the Neolithic period are still to be found in the contemporary era.

On the other hand it is true that, apart from the documentation provided by the frescoes on the walls of Çatal Hüyük, dating from as far back as the sixth millennium BC, there are no elements (with rare exceptions that will be discussed further on) attesting to the continuity of the presence of these figurative themes.

What happened to the kilims in the meantime? There are no sure answers to this question, but I believe that women continued to weave them for domestic and personal use, using a technique passed on from mother to daughter, over the generations. Support for this hypothesis of mine comes, in the first place, from the consideration that the material of the kilim was subject to rapid deterioration as a result of the constant and casual use to which they were put. People walked, slept and ate on kilims; kilims were beds for children;

they were exposed to dust and bad weather; they were loaded, as baggage, on beasts of burden. Being neither commercial products nor art objects, they were utilitarian articles, subject to daily wear and tear, and replaced as they wore out.

Another consideration can be brought in in support of the hypothesis of the continuity of their manufacture over the course of time: how would it have been possible for the kilims woven in the last three centuries to have the same design as those depicted at Çatal Hüyük if their tradition and memory had been lost for more than seven thousand years?

Naturally, in the absence of documentary proof, these are only suppositions, but in my opinion they are highly plausible. If we accept the hypothesis of their continuity in time, which I have been proposing for many years and which now seems to be the prevailing view among experts, the tradition of the kilim survived notwithstanding the transformation of culture, the succession of invasions and rulers, changes in religion and language, and economic and social upheavals. Everything changed, but the culture of the kilim rode the crest of the wave down to our own day, mysteriously preserved from the waters of time. Why? When the culture of the Mother Goddess gave way first to the polytheistic religions and then to the monotheistic ones of Judaism, Christianity and Islam, when Anatolia turned from a country with no fortresses into a theater of war and conquest, when the Turks arrived from the East and the Christians from the West, when the reign of money began, with the exploitation of slaves and the oppression of women: when all this happened in Anatolia and everything changed, according to the rules of logic those symbols ought to have changed as well. According to the rules of logic. But we have to take into account the ex-

istence of other factors that, in certain cases, constitute insurmountable bulwarks in defense of a manifestation of human culture. And, from what has been said so far, we can assert that these bulwarks should be sought not *outside* but *inside* the human soul.

If the archetypal language arises out of the unconscious and tends to produced images with a collective value, it will not run dry and cease to produce them, insofar as it remains active and viable in the psyche. Evidently, over the course of time, the woven patterns in kilims kept alive an unconscious inner dialogue between the women of Anatolia and their foremothers, a dialogue that can be generically defined as tradition. If you ask weavers today why they always repeat the same motifs on their kilims they invariably respond *anane*, which means tradition in Turkish and, at the same time (phonetically) "from mother to daughter." Of course they do not know why they repeat those figures, but they do know that the reason lies in a tradition that links women together in a chain stretching back nine thousand years. And so it is in tradition that the meaning lies, and the meaning—as we have seen—is unconscious.

If a contemporary human being dreams of a labyrinth, for example, as an unconscious message of the endlessness of the cycle of life, the women of Anatolia represented it, wide awake. This means that those weavers, almost always illiterate and compelled to live a very harsh life, were closer than us to the archetypal images of the collective unconscious, perhaps precisely because they were more primitive.

It often happens, moreover, that words or feelings that are extraordinary profound and an expression of a universal truth come from very simple people, lacking in what is usually called *culture*. This is no accident, for these people, in the absence of other means, retain a much stronger tie with general and profound truths and sometimes find a way to express them.

I have been told a story by a friend who, during a long stay in Afghanistan in the seventies, happened to meet an elderly nomad in a tent in the desert to the north of Kandahar, the only member of his tribe who spoke a little English. At a certain point a cat ran into the tent and curled up on a small chest. She asked the old man "Is that your cat?" and he answered "It is its own cat." It is impossible to know to what extent that man was conscious of having said that no one is ever master of another, not even of an animal, because what defines a being is its autonomy and therefore its own law. We cannot know how aware the old man was of what he had said, but he said it.

Going back to the kilims, I find it easy to understand how this tradition survived thanks to the monopoly of weaving by women, in part because the images refer to the force and majesty of the Mother Goddess, while all around them was emerging a social context that belittled and humiliated women. The figures of the kilims were repeated because they constituted a sort of *free zone* in which the collective unconscious continued to weave its own truth, outside of time, founded on the wisdom of the maternal principle and on its immense creative energy.

In view of what has been said so far, I consider the ideas put forward by some scholars to explain the extraordinary continuity of the Anatolian kilim to be incidental and not in themselves convincing. Belkis Balpinar, for example, suggests that the isolated existence of the Anatolian communities, which were not subject to movement or break-up, would have allowed them to retain the repertory of designs intact down the generations.[9] Similarly Udo Hirsch ascribes the phenomenon to the strong sense of tribal allegiance of the Anatolian peoples. "Due to the unchanging group way of life," he writes, "and the profound collective opposition to any type of change, the weavers of each generation perpetuate to a great extent what has been handed down to them by the previous generation."[10] It is his opinion, as a consequence, that kilims from different tribal groups have markedly different characteristics. These considerations throw some light on the phenomenon but are, in my view, insufficient to explain it. Over the course of human history there have been many other cases of tribes, whether settled or nomadic, remaining isolated without them ever having kept alive images from the Neolithic period down to our own day. It is true that there are some differences between the kilims produced by different tribal groups, although in my view they are not substantial. We should not forget, however, that these articles have a history that goes back several thousand years before the formation of the tribes that we know today.

Still seeking an explanation for the millennia of apparent silence from the kilims, James Mellaart has made some comments that I consider to be of great importance and worth quoting in full: "These woven relics of a lost religion are a splendid testimony to something which was already old when writing appeared soon after 2000 BC; it needs little imagination to see the palaces and mansions of kings and nobles from the third to the first millennia BC decorated with kilims four to five meters in length. Among the historical peoples of Anatolia known to us from texts were Ilattians and Hittites, Hurrians, Luvians, Arzawans and their descendants and successors such as Phrygians, Lydians, Lycians, Cilicians, Lycaonians, Pisidians and so on; if our theory is correct, Anatolian kilims will give us at least a glimpse of the lost ornamental textiles of these peoples.

"The size alone of such textiles suggests that this art form was not created for village rooms or tents but to cover the walls of large chambers, where their compositions could be clearly seen and their meanings understood. This would also explain why no traces of other decoration—wall paintings and reliefs in wood or stone—have ever been found in the interiors of Anatolian palaces and mansions from the third to the first millennia BC. As we have noted in the previous chapter, peg holes occur in the walls of the richest shrines at Çatal Hüyük and they are also found in the great hall of the Gordion palace, which dates from the eighth century BC, roughly the time of Midas. Imprints of slit-tapestry occur in the plaster walls at Çatal Hüyük; burned fragments of cloth were found stuck to the pegs at Gordion where fragments of kilims, although carbonized, have survived both in the palace and the tombs. "In Phrygia, monumental open air shrines of Cybele, the chief goddess, are concentrated in an area around Midas City, north of Afyon Karahisar. Many of these shrines have geometric decoration in carved stone around the niches of statues which strongly recall textile patterns; rural shrines presumably made use of actual textiles.

"The patterns which have survived from the Phrygian period are not those of our kilims; this does not present a real obstacle to our thesis, however, since examples are limited in number and Phrygian art can be described as the 'court art' of a non-Anatolian ruling class; some of the patterns recur, however, on Anatolian village rugs.

Greek sources—there are no native Phrygian ones—single out the practices of Phrygian religion as orgiastic and unorthodox, involving acts of self-castration, something not encountered in the earlier Hittite texts. Other foreign cults were introduced by later conquerors—the Persians, Greeks, Galatians (Celts) and Romans.

With the arrival of Christianity and Islam, the Old Religion gradually withered and the message of the kilims was no longer understood; ironically, this undoubtedly ensured their survival, as they were considered merely as the harmless rags of peasants and pastoralists, a non-urban and illiterate population. Ancient household gods on household goods, for such the kilims were, did not attract attention, offered no provocation and were thus no cause for political concern. The attitude of the Islamic establishment toward them is aptly summed up in the expression 'cheap and nasty.'"[11]

So Mellaart is putting forward the hypothesis that, at a certain moment, when monumental architecture began to appear in Anatolia, the tradition of the kilim reached a fork in the road: on the one hand the tribal or village rug with its utilitarian and religious ties continued undisturbed along its modest course, passing silently from generation to generation without leaving any trace behind it, and on the other the *art kilims*, used to decorate the palaces of the powerful, the only ones who were in a position to grasp its symbolic dimension, have left some traces in the form of descriptions in books and a few documentary records. The former were made to be used and consumed, the latter to be looked at and preserved. It is no surprise, then, with the divergent course taken by the two kinds of kilims, and the consequent difference in the significance attributed to them, that the patterns and designs of the one bore no more than a partial resemblance to those of the other. I think that all I need to add, in this connection, is that, precisely for the reasons given by Mellaart, the kilims linked to the Anatolian tradition of use are the ones that should be regarded as *classic kilims*. For, as we have seen, it is not necessary for people to know the meaning of a symbol in order to feel it alive and at work within

them, and this is particularly true where, as in this case, it was the women who actually wove them, keeping the tradition alive. The fact is that a tradition does not stay alive because it is understood, but because it is seen as necessary, because it forms an integral part of the personality of the person who hands it down. Commercial kilims, or those produced for decoration or the courts, may have been preserved, but it was the spirit and significance of the classic kilims that survived, as is demonstrated by the frescoes of Çatal Hüyük. So my position diverges from that of Mellaart when he writes: "Alternately old features can easily be preserved in mountain areas and it is in this way that I would like to explain how Neolithic religious symbols could have survived for thousands of years and reemerge in Anatolian kilims of the seventeenth–nineteenth century, having lost their meaning but not their shape."[12]

As I have already pointed out, isolation in itself does not explain the phenomenon. What is more, on the basis of the foregoing pages, I cannot do otherwise than stress that kilims were able to survive for such a long time *precisely* because they had not lost their underlying significance and therefore their form as well. The fact that this meaning was unknown to the conscious mind does not alter my argument. On the contrary, it supports it since, as analytical psychology has demonstrated, unconscious contents are not infrequently the most deeply rooted and constant elements of human behavior.

In the second place, the archetypal meaning of the designs and structure of kilims did not become unconscious at a particular moment, but had always been so since the women (who were members of a tribe, or of the community of a village or town) wove, for example, a spiral or a double meander because it was a form that mysteriously belonged to them, and not because they

were aware that that pattern *had something to say* about the cycle of eternal recurrence. The childhood of the human being, from this point of view, is no different from the childhood of the human race.

[1] J. Mellaart, *Dove nacque la civiltà*, Italian edition, Newton Compton, Rome, 1981, p. 16. (Original title: *The Archaeology of Ancient Turkey*).
[2] J. Mellaart, op. cit., pp. 16-19.
[3] J. Mellaart, op. cit., p. 23.
[4] So-called from the name of the closest modern locality.
[5] J. Mellaart, op. cit., p. 16.
[6] J. Mellaart, quoted in D. Valcarenghi, "Il valore simbolico nella mitologia del kilim," in *Kilim anatolici*, Electa, Milan 1985, p. 15.
[7] D. Valcarenghi, "Il valore simbolico nella mitologia del kilim," in op. cit.
[8] J. Thompson, *The Undiscovered Kilim*, David Black, London 1977; J. Petsopoulos, *Les Kilims*, Edition Vilo, Paris 1979; B. Balpinar, *The Goddess from Anatolia*, Eskenazi, Milan 1989, vol. IV; J. Mellaart, *The Goddess from Anatolia*, op. cit., vol. II.
[9] B. Balpinar, op. cit., vol. IV.
[10] U. Hirsch, "I gruppi tribali anatolici e i loro kilim," in *Kilim anatolici*, op. cit. p. 50.
[11] J. Mellaart, *The Goddess from Anatolia*, op. cit., vol. II, p. 50.
[12] J. Mellaart, *Early Turkish Tapestries*, B. Frauenknecht, Nuremberg 1984, p. 32.

The Representation of Original Ambivalence

There is a Middle-Eastern saying dating from the fourteenth century that runs "everyone can pull his own kilim out of the water."[1] A way of saying many things and, at bottom, only one: we could interpret it as "everyone can find their own submerged roots," or "everyone can recover their own lost identity," or even "everyone can dig out their own truth from the unconscious." Given that I too am trying to pull my kilim out of the water, I cannot help but point out once again that the investigation and understanding of symbols do not follow a rational course, but an analogical one; not a deductive course, but an inductive one. As Jung reminds us: "an image is symbolic when it implies something that goes beyond its obvious and immediate meaning. It possesses a broader, unconscious aspect, that is never defined with precision or completely explained. Nor can one hope to define or explain it. When the mind explores the symbol, it is brought into contact with ideas that lies outside the capacities of the rational mind."[2]

As an image gradually starts to *speak*, we realize that the analogies and the different messages remain linked together in a tension that tends to spread. In addition, and no differently from words, the images interact, creating a dynamic and complex meaning, as vital as the flow of a discourse, only to go back and conceal themselves in the end behind the motionless signs through which they found expression.

Duality: the most deeply rooted, most widespread and most constant symbol to be found in the design of the kilim concerns the structure of the textile itself. In fact, two threads are twisted together in the spinning of the yarn, the loom—as we saw in the previous chapter—has two coordinates, and the woven rug itself is made up of two symmetrical parts. And finally, there are two images in every design, depending on whether it is seen in negative or positive. Let us take a closer look at these last two aspects with the help of figure 3. It is immediately obvious that this rug is made up of two pieces of cloth sewn together lengthwise: the two parts are symmetrical and make up a whole. This feature, a relatively constant one in classic kilims (whether or not they are sewn together) can already be seen in the wall paintings of Çatal Hüyük (fig. 4) and is even mentioned in Ovid's *Metamorphoses*, where he speaks of the weaver's *geminae telae* (twin cloths): out of their union is born the fabric, whose variously colored images represent "the variegated rug of the earth."[3]

Even today many experts still believe that this peculiarity of the twin cloths is a consequence of the small size of the loom, which made it necessary to weave the rug in two stages. My hypothesis, on the other hand, is based on the analogy of this dualism with the other aspects of the same principle that have already been referred to and which, taken altogether, serve to demonstrate the need of the weavers to speak of the ambivalence they perceived in everything. The two parts of a kilim are always very similar and "related" to one another, but they are never exactly the same, in much the same way as in the image of the human body, for instance, the right-hand side and the left-hand side are *almost* the same, but not identical. I feel that an important part of the fascination of a kilim lies in just this peculiar equilibrium, based on analogies, assonances and dissonances, rather than on a rigid and impersonal identity.

In Turkey I have heard tell of an ancient custom, which seems to have vanished during the last century, of cutting kilims in half for reasons of inheritance. Confirmation of this tradition seems to come from a number of examples that have survived, but these kilims had not been divided along the longitudinal seam, which would have resulted in two symmetrically similar pieces of

3. Kilim cat. 36.

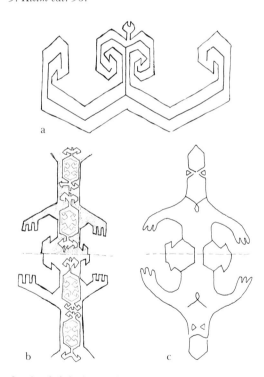

3a. Symbol depicting the goddess seated with legs apart present in the kilim.
3b. Image of the goddess gripping two vultures by the necks: these symbols can be seen in the kilim shown above.
3c. Detail of wall painting found at Çatal Hüyük.

fabric, but across the kilim so as to leave each of the heirs half of each element of the design. It is possible to see this choice as a recognition of the intangibility of the dual symbol, as if to underline the fact that unity does not lie in one, but in two.

Looking at figure 3 (reproduced in color in the catalogue) and, at the same time, drawing 3*a*, we are able to see another interesting aspect of duality in kilims: the positive-negative double image. We can make out in the rug, in fact, a highly stylized representation of the goddess, depicted three times in each of the two symmetrical halves. In the first and in the third image (blue and red) can be seen a small head, arms bent inward and legs wide apart and crooked. But it is also possible to recognize another goddess in *negative* in the white part of the kilim, as can be seen more clearly in drawing *b*. Drawing *c* shows the same image as drawing *b* (in negative in the kilim) and is taken from a fresco at Çatal Hüyük.

In the two wall paintings reproduced in figure 5 the negative images of the goddess are particularly evident. In the first painting, starting from the top, we

see a pale yellow figure and a pink one in the first row and a beige figure and a brown one in the second row. All four of them have blue horns. In the second fragment there are two figures in negative, one dappled yellow and one red, both with horns and a steatopygous form. The duality, in this fragment, is also represented by the double figures of animals, a recurrent theme in kilims and in the most ancient iconography in general.

In figure 3 the negative and the positive are also visible in the blue patterns (black in negative) woven on the short borders and in the black patterns (red in negative) woven on the longer sides. Sometimes the positive and negative images are related to one another, as in figure 3 (which should be compared with drawing *c*) where the two bird's heads are woven in positive; in contrast, the body of the goddess and the two hands holding them are in negative.

Continuing with our examination of figure 3 (emblematic of innumerable similar rugs), we can see the stylization of the white goddess in negative, gripping two bird's heads.

The image is easy to recognize if the

4. *Çatal Hüyük.*
Reconstruction of wall
painting with mirror images
of deities.

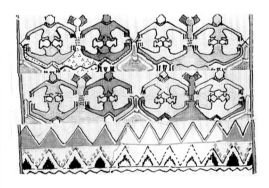

5. *Çatal Hüyük.*
Reconstruction of wall
painting with deities and
animals.

kilim is compared with the detail of a fresco from Çatal Hüyük (fig. 6*a*) and with the detail from another kilim (fig. 6*b*), where once again it is possible to see two bent arms with stylized hands gripping the necks of the two birds with bowed heads.

The last element of duality can be found in the two symbols that often appear alongside the goddess. In figure 3 they are visible—represented in more or less the same colors—alongside the two blue and red divine images and the central green and violet one. This expression of duality can take different forms, such as a stylized bull's head, a geometric pattern, or an anthropomorphic figure, but is usually located at the sides of the goddess's head. This can clearly be seen in figure 7 with its enormous bull's head depicted in a realistic manner.

Other images of feminine duality can be found in figure 8: here the two symmetrical halves are clearly visible, but equally evident is the repetition of the dual symbol of the double-headed axe, a tool with two blades. This appears several times in the frescoes at Çatal Hüyük and can be found in all the oldest cultures of the Middle-Eastern basin and Crete. We see it represented in the form of the symmetrically composed double triangle on the white ground of the kilim and woven in various colors (green, red and green, blue, blue and red, yellow, red and yellow, and so on) along with many small crosses and other geometric figures. The double-headed axe is recognizable in figure 9, reproducing a detail from a fresco at Çatal Hüyük. In figure 8 duality also puts in an appearance in the stylized head, looking like a sort of double *wrench*, also woven in different colors on the white ground of the rug and repeated on the borders.

It should come as no surprise that the image of a stylized head recurs in countless kilims from different periods. The theme is already apparent in figure 4, where two horns are clearly visible on the head of the goddess. And this attribute appears rarely in kilims in a different way *from the wrench-shaped head*. In figures 10*a* and *b* we find the image of stylized horns turned upward and downward: the resemblance with that of the goddess in the Çatal Hüyük fresco seen in figure 4 is obvious.

6a. *Çatal Hüyük.*
Stylization of the goddess
gripping two vultures; detail
taken from a wall painting.
6b. *Stylization of the goddess*
gripping two vultures; detail
taken from a kilim (cat. 37).
6c. *Stylization of the goddess*
gripping two vultures; detail
taken from a kilim (cat. 94).
6d. *Abstraction of the symbol*
of the goddess repeated in the
lateral band of a nineteenth-
century kilim. The four
images show how progressive
stylization of the body of the
goddess, whose open arms
form a cross, has led to the
representation of a cross
alone.
6e. *Symbol of the vultures*
repeated in the lateral band
of a nineteenth-century kilim.
6f. *Çatal Hüyük.*
Detail with vultures taken
from a wall painting dating
from 6600 BC.

a b

c d

e f

Moreover stylized heads, equipped with horns or in the shape of a horn, are a characteristic of both the Neolithic iconography and the more recent cultures of the Mediterranean basin. Finally we come to the double meander, woven in red and black respectively on the borders of the short sides of the kilim in figure 3: this is a dual image that we find in numerous kilims, as well as in a great deal of ancient iconog-

raphy from all over the world. The double meander lies at the origin of more complex images such as the swastika and the labyrinth. An example of this can be seen, for example, in figure 11. As we have seen, the dual principle is represented in a constant and almost obsessive manner in the designs of kilims. Why? What was the origin of these dual images? To what demands were they a response? What kind of awareness did they express?

There was once a time when human beings, just like other animals, were not aware of their existence: they lived and died, but were unconscious of living and dying; they were immersed in nature, and nature contained the whole existence of the human race. Just as the fetus in the mother's womb and the newborn baby place their trust completely in the mother and identify themselves with her totally, the human race, at the dawn of time, identified with nature in a relationship of defenseless and needy dependence.

This was the unconscious phase in the history of humanity, corresponding, on the level of analogy, with the life of the fetus and the first few months of infancy. At this time human beings did not think or say *I* and therefore did not think or say *you* either: there was no

7. *Çatal Hüyük.*
Reconstruction of wall
painting with figures of the
goddess and bull's heads.

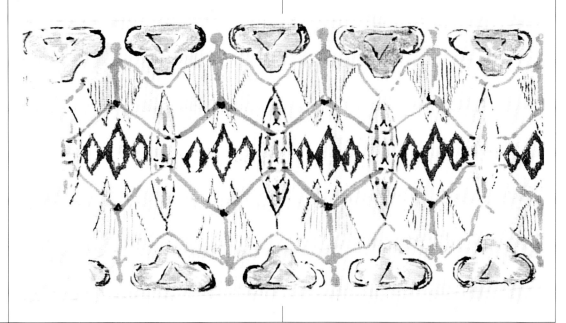

8. *Images of duality repeated in a kilim (cat. 47).*

9. *Çatal Hüyük. Copy of a fresco showing the double-headed axe often to be found in both kilims and paintings.*

separation because there was no consciousness, and so there was no creator because there was no creature. This is a lost world that only returns in sleep and death, but once humanity lived in it and the child still lives in it prior to becoming self aware.

The unconscious phase of history came to an end on the day when for the first time someone thought and said: *I*. The rest was then *automatically* differentiated. Human beings felt themselves to have been expelled from the womb of nature and became aware of the limits of their *ego*.

This marked the definitive break with the original condition of the ouroboros,[4] the closed circle of an unconscious totality, in the same way in which the cutting of the umbilical cord marks the definitive separation of child from mother.

This early form of consciousness, elementary but still fundamental, committed humanity to awareness and solitude. It was the time when the indistinct whole came to an end and the one was split into two. *I exist and therefore the world exists, I and all the rest, I and you*: it

was the beginning of every dichotomy and every dialectic, the start of all knowledge. It was also the origin of history and of culture, for if the universe is different from us, then we have no choice but to try and understand it, describe it, and conquer it.

But the first *you* that the human being met was *nature*, just as the first *you* that the child meets is the *mother*, that is she who contained it and from whom it has been separated. In this sense the analogy between nature and the mother has always been perceived as relevant and necessary. At the dawn of civilization nature was seen as the Great Mother, capable of exercising almost unlimited power over human life.

Over the course of history, human intelligence has, little by little, penetrated the laws of nature and deciphered its signals. It has gradually succeeded in understanding nature and, to a certain extent, controlling it. In the first part of that course, however, the maternal divinity, the first one that the human race felt the need to name and to worship, represented the union of opposites, the mysterious energy from which every-

10. Detail of kilim cat. 50.

10a. b. Mirror images of stylized horns at the top of the goddess's head which can be seen in the kilim.
10c. Detail of the double-headed axe held by the headless goddess in the kilim.

11. Kilim cat. 134.

11a. Symbol of the double S (swastika) as it appears in the kilim reproduced above.
11b. Symbol of the double S (meander) that appears on the bands of kilim cat. 110.

thing originates and to which everything returns and which exercises absolute power over everything.

The *I* was still fragile, while the *you* was overpowering. Interiorized as mother, it contained within itself all the knowable aspects of reality and therefore all the pairs of opposites, just like the biological mother who gives birth to both the female and the male. So the Mother Goddess is, at one and the same time, sleeping and waking, heat and cold, inside and outside, light and dark, life and death, and—as will be shown more clearly later on—man and woman.

Two, therefore, as image of all ambivalence, lies at the origin of the first consciousness, the one from which all the others derive.

When the human being began to observe, name, and understand the sensible world, the pairs of opposites referred solely to natural situations (heat, cold, light, dark and so on). But when thought started to grow more complex and to reflect on itself, the pairs of opposites began to define the world of the soul, and out of this came good and evil, passion and fear, before and after, the ephemeral and the eternal...

So we can understand Bachofen when he writes: "In this linking of becoming with being, of the earthly world with the celestial one, of movement with immobility, of the world of the living with that of the dead, of the sensible world with the super-sensible world, lies the highest spiritual content of the ancient religion of nature, and this spiritualization is all the greater an achievement given the closeness of its affinity with matter itself."[5]

But if two separates the opposites and, at the same time, contains them, it is understandable that it should also represent totality and, consequently, the infinite. Good and evil together constitute a whole that, *as such*, has no bounds.

Today we assign a very different value to the concept of infinity, one that is bound up with personal knowledge and with scientific, moral and philosophical convictions. But at the time of the Great Goddess the infinite was exclusively natural, interwoven with the manifestations of the sensible world and enclosed within the cycle of eternal recurrence. Night and day, distinct but regarded as one, were infinite since they never came to an end and one always gave rise to the other. It was the same with life and death and with the alternation of the seasons, the tides and the phases of the moon. This is why comprehension of the opposites in duality lies at the root of the continual, eternal, infinite transformation of the whole that was expressed in the culture of the Mother Goddess by the swastika or the double meander and that was to reemerge in Greek philosophy in the form of Heraclitus' synthesis: *panta rhei* [all things are in a flux].

[1] B. Balpinar, *The Goddess from Anatolia*, Eskenazi, Milan 1989, vol. IV, p. 4.
[2] C. G. Jung, *Man and His Symbols*, Aldus Books Ltd., London 1967.
[3] Ovid, *Metamorphoses*, 6, 54.
[4] The ouroboros is the coiled serpent that bites its own tail. This image, which represents the archetype of the original psychic unity, the preconscious condition of humanity, appears not only in myths and in ancient iconography, but also in the dreams of contemporary people.
The original psychic unity refers to that stage in evolution in which the whole of reality was still contained within the closed circle of the tension of opposites: the ouroboros is at one and the same time male and female, beginning and end, light and shade, and so on. This phase occurred prior to the development of individual consciousness, at a time when humanity was still rolled up in the circle of the totality of nature.
[5] J. J. Bachofen, *Il simbolismo funerario degli antichi*, Italian edition, Guida, Naples 1989, p. 505.

The Body of the Goddess

The body of the goddess, the chief figure of the Anatolian kilims, can assume more or less stylized forms, be complicated by hyperanthropic motifs, and exercise different functions. It is, in any case, a dominant presence that reasserts the maternal principle as the mysterious source of all forms of fertility and of all transformation.

A prayer to Isis, supreme goddess of ancient Egypt, runs: "I am the mother of the whole of nature, mistress of all the elements, origin and beginning of time, supreme divinity, first among the inhabitants of heaven, origin of the gods and goddesses. The luminous heights of the sky, the salubrious breath of the sea, the desolate silences of the nether world, it is I who governs them all according to my will."

These words convey the profound meaning of the goddess of origins and everything that I will have to say about her in the kilims is no more than an extension and exemplification of the images to be found in this prayer. In the first place, the goddess is a hermaphrodite and from the viewpoint of the study of the symbol it would, in my view, be a grave error to confuse her with the feminine principle.

She is the unique source of the archetypes of gods and goddesses, the *arché* of both, at one and the same time receptive and phallic, solar and lunar. In much more recent epochs of history, the Great Mother was split into god and goddess and, at an even later stage, the two archetypes were broken up into a series of divinities with different names and functions. In the Egyptian religion, for example, Geb, Os, Osiris and Set are four male divinities with specific attributes; the same is true for Hermes, Apollo, Dionysius and Zeus in Greek culture and, among the female divinities, Demeter, Aphrodite, Artemis, Athene and so on. In the distant past, however, this separation had not yet taken place and the goddess was one, man and woman together. Without taking into account this concept, familiar to anyone interested in symbology and the history of religions, it would be impossible to make sense of the many images from the Paleolithic and Neolithic periods in which the symbols of the phallus and the vagina are represented together (figs. 12 and 13). We would not be able to understand why Isis is so often depicted with the sun and two crescent moons on her head, or why the neck of the statue of Cybele, the original Great Goddess of Asia Minor, should be adorned with a necklace made of the penises of the priests emasculated in her honor.

The examples that can be cited in support of the hermaphroditism of the original divinity are innumerable. Moreover traces of the splitting of the hermaphrodite goddess have survived in mythologies with which we are familiar, such as the Greek myth about the birth of Cybele: this relates that Cybele was born in Greece from the sperm of Zeus (in this way she was *nationalized* and turned from a mother into a daughter). She was, however, born as a hermaphrodite, arousing horror and dismay on the part of the Lords of Olympus, who therefore decided to emasculate her and turn her into a female nature divinity. Stripped of her potency in this way, they accepted her presence among them.

The bisexual dimension is detectable in the frescoes of Çatal Hüyük and, in a stylized form, in the design of a good many kilims. In figure 6*a*, for instance, we see the goddess equipped with horns and obvious male sexual organs. In figure 14 we can see that the gray images in negative, unlike the upper, paler ones, have external sexual attributes. In the kilim in figure 16 and, more analytically, in the detail in drawing *a*, we see how, of the four forms at the sides of the goddess, the two lower ones have head, body, arms and legs, while the two upper ones (symmetrical and therefore turned upside down) have head, body, arms, legs and an extension of the body that can be regarded as a phallic shape. The maternal divinity was male and female not only because the woman gives birth to the male as well as the female, and because in the remote past human beings were not aware of the male's power to fecundate, but also because in the manifestations of nature, starting with the four elements air, water, earth and fire, receptive and penetrative modes of acting were recognizable. Water *penetrates* the earth, which *receives* it. Fire *penetrates* the forest, air *holds* the birds, the clouds and the stars, the flower *receives* the bee and so on in a duality of always interconnected functions that serve to reproduce the eternal cycle of changes. In view of all the foregoing considerations, I am led to think that the phallic symbols in Anatolian kilims—even though not realistically sexual—have their symbolic origin in the sexual duality of the goddess.

In kilims—as in all the most ancient iconography—the goddess is very often seated: in Anatolian kilims her legs are usually spread to the point where they form a horizontal line, as can be seen in the bas-relief from Çatal Hüyük reproduced in figure 15 and in the fragment of a wall decoration in figure 14. It is in this position that the six principal divinities in figure 3 are represented (as was pointed out in the previous chapter), as well as in figure 16, where we see slender figures with their legs spread and images of the great goddess in red, blue and violet (see cat. 104). In my opinion the two positions—seated and seated with the legs apart—have independent symbolic meanings. The term *possess*, of Indo-European origin and derived from the Latin *possidere*, can be said to be made up of *posse*, which means *to be able* and *sed*, which refers to the seated position. Thus from an etymological

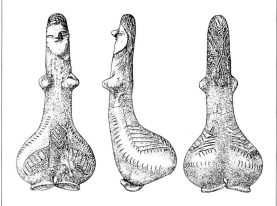

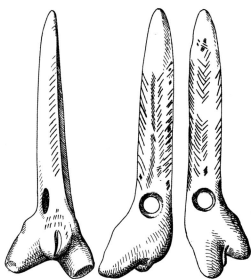

12. 13. Figures combining male and female sexual symbols.

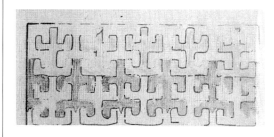

14. Çatal Hüyük. Reconstruction of wall painting with images in positive and negative of the goddess, whose legs are spread until they form a horizontal line.

Opposite page:
15. Çatal Hüyük. Relief depicting the goddess with legs spread.

point of view the verb to possess appears to signify *to be able—to sit*, but it also means to exercise control, dominion, authority. So it would appear that the seated position has been a symbol of power and social importance ever since the most ancient of times.

I think it is no different with the kilims: the divinity is seated on the whole of the sensible world, represented by the set of other symbolic images beneath her: the cave, the double-headed axe, the spiral, the swastika, the rhombus, the cross, water, earth and everything that belongs to her because it is from her that it has taken form and life.

The seated position with the legs spread, which displays the sexual organs, takes on a whole range of meaning connected with sexual and reproductive energy. The sexual aspect of symbols is usually the one least noticed in a sex phobic culture of Christian inspiration but, at a time when people were not condemned to hell for having made love and were not made into saints for having blinded themselves at the sight of a penis,[1] the pleasure was sacred and the object of worship.

It is not difficult to imagine that the wholly irrational and mysterious component that regulates the biological and psychic aspect of sexuality made a great impression on our remote ancestors, convincing them of the magical and religious power of the various aspects of sexual life.

Moreover it would be over simplistic to link sexuality too closely with reproduction: Neolithic peoples, as I have already mentioned, made no connection between coitus and any pregnancy that might result; sexual pleasure was seen as something that had a value of its own, as a divine gift. So in the kilim the figure of the legs spread wide speaks of both pleasure and fertility, with connections stretching back to times when orgiastic rites were practiced as part of the cult of blood.

In all the kilims reproduced in this book it is possible to see a curved shape at the base of the goddess's body. Sometimes made up of concentric rhombuses, this shape occasionally contains other symbols but, as a whole, refers to the egg, to pregnancy, to birth, to what grows in the cave, in the mountain, in the earth, in the womb and then comes to light as metal, grain, or child.[2]

Yet the goddess does not just preside over births: as a symbol of nature it causes birth and death, for it contains within it the mystery of the seed that decomposes in the darkness of the earth and that, precisely because it dies, will return from the earth to germinate. There is no life without birth, and there is no life without death. This awareness led to the recognition of the divinity as mistress of both, arbitress of eternal recurrence. Another function of the goddess as represented in the kilims concerns her dominion over vultures. Looking at figures 6*a* and *b*, we see the divinity gripping two birds by their necks. We know that they are vultures because the frescoes at Çatal Hüyük depicting the burial ritual show the dead body being exposed to vultures on a sort of altar. It is certainly true that the two birds, as in many other designs, are a symbol of duality, but what do they mean *in particular*? And what does their control by the goddess mean? If the birds devoured the remains of the dead, they must have been seen as the transforming agents of death, the terrible but necessary energy that wipes out the traces of existence, that purifies death and therefore permits regeneration. Being mistress of the vultures may have meant exercising undisputed and acknowledged sway over an energy that is destructive, terrible and dark, but as necessary as the creative energy to maintaining the balance of the biological cycle. No wonder that, in the oldest cultures, human beings should have attributed to the maternal divinity knowledge of and dominion over the forces that were beyond their control in daily life. This is the reason why, quite apart from the symbolic value of indi-

vidual animals in a given culture, vultures, lions, eagles, leopards, bulls, wolves and snakes have been depicted at the feet of gods, even in civilizations very distant from one another. Humans were afraid of these animals that were stronger than themselves, being vulnerable to their violence, their poison and their claws. The animals, in turn, were subject to a natural law of which they knew nothing but which the human being was able to sense and gradually come to understand.

In the Anatolian tradition, as in almost all the religions of the Mother Goddess, the bull had a profound and complex totemic significance. This significance filtered from the wall paintings of Çatal Hüyük into the patterns of weaving, retaining all of its vitality. The horns of the bull, fused and interlaced with other images, are to be found in very many kilims: they are concealed in the body of the goddess, they can be recognized in the double meander, or they appear beneath a triangle, becoming one of the dominant motifs of the iconography of the woven rug. A deep ambivalence lurks in the bull: it is male for its sexual vigor, the abundance of its semen, and the strength of its body, female for its roundish curves, its color of the earth and its horns (always highly evident in the iconography) that link it to the phases of the moon, the night and therefore the fertility of nature. The ambivalent image of the bull expresses the exuberance of the fertilizing energy united with an extraordinary destructive fury in a dualism in which the people of the remote past must have recognized a fundamental law of nature. Let us try, for example, to imagine a human being of that time under a starry sky, sitting in a meadow filled with flowers, or by a calm summer sea teeming with fish, and then picture the same person faced with an earthquake, caught in a storm or a fire, or threatened by a grumbling volcano: the feel-

16. Kilim cat. 104.

a

b

16a. Stylizations of the steatopygous goddess with figures with bisexual attributes at the sides, taken from the kilim reproduced above.

16b. Çatal Hüyük. Detail of a wall painting with figures with bisexual attributes.

17. Statue from the third millennium BC representing a goddess in the guise of a bull holding a vase. The tuning-fork symbols on her dress are common in Anatolian kilims (cats. 65 and 139).

ing of duality must have been as mysterious as it was alarming, but in any case tangible. If the fundamental characteristic of the bull is its dualism and if this characteristic is also that of nature, then it is comprehensible why all the religions of the great mother were founded on the cult of the bull. Anatolians, Sumerians, Egyptians, Cretans, Syrians, Jews, Babylonians, and Phoenicians all kneeled in worship of images of an animal that was nothing but a representation of the Mother Goddess.

Such an assumption helps to explain the extraordinary persistence and longevity of this symbol in a variety of cultures, including far more recent ones: the Jewish patriarchs who migrated to Palestine, for instance, still practiced the cult of the bull El, which was supposed to have been forbidden by Moses but which survived at least until the reign of David.

Another example of the vitality of the symbol of the bull can be found in a myth related by Hesiod. In a culture that was by this time clearly patriarchal, Zeus, the father of the gods, fell in love with Europa, a girl who lived in Libya. To seduce her he turned himself into a marvelous white bull, approached her and lay down at her feet. The trusting Europa caressed the animal and

climbed onto his back. At this point the bull set off at a gallop and carried the girl across Syria, Anatolia and the Bosphorus, until they came to Crete. Here he allowed the young woman to descend and united with her, siring three children and giving rise to the first European civilization on that island. This

28

myth does not just tell us about the Middle Eastern origin of the Cretan civilization, but also about the importance that Greek culture, at that time, assigned to the bull.

In the second century of our era, an ancient Babylonian initiation rite, ascribable to the cult of Cybele, established itself in Rome, where it was known by the name of *taurobolium*. The person to be initiated descended into a specially dug pit. This was then covered with a plank full of large holes, on top of which a bull's throat was cut. The warm blood flowed through the holes onto the naked body of the man in the pit. Anyone who underwent this bloody aspersion was *renatus in aeternum*, that is born into a new life for eternity. The blood, as a symbol of energy and life, was, no less than the bull, a dual symbol: male as the origin of physical strength and vitality, female as the cyclic flow linked with birth. During the *taurobolium*, the ambivalent nature of the bull's vital force made it possible to become part of the cycle of death and rebirth, the cycle of eternal recurrence as it had been known in the "Eleusinian mysteries."

So it is easy to understand how the tradition of the kilim, an offshoot of the ancient Anatolian culture, uses the motif of the bull almost as if it were a connective element for the whole of the symbology, the extreme stylization of a fundamental *double* that had accompanied humanity in its journey out of the original chaos and toward consciousness. Writing of the Great Mother as a symbol of fertility, J. Mellaart says: "[...] the only functions of female deities in both wall paintings and kilims are to give birth and, by so doing, to set examples of fertility and regeneration for the world they govern. The message comes over loud and clear, even from the dim past of the upper Paleolithic; and since it is still understood, its emphasis on continuity through millennia of time has been comprehended by

18. Detail of kilim cat. 70.

18a. Hyperanthropic figures taken from the kilim reproduced here. The last image is taken from kilim cat. 75.

18b. Hyperanthropic figures from the Paleolithic period.

a

b

29

even the least gifted of us—life must go on and there is no other way of ensuring it than procreation. The appeal of such a religion was clearly instantaneous; no later religion has ever been able to suppress it, even if individuals or sects have sometimes chosen celibacy."[3]

At the cost of passing for the "least gifted of us," I do not feel able, in this case, to agree wholeheartedly with the distinguished scholar. In view of what has been said so far, the functions of the maternal divinity in the iconography of Çatal Hüyük and the kilims seem to be far more complex than mere procreation. Frequently, in the kilim, it is possible to recognize *hyperanthropic* motifs in the body of the goddess: this is the name given by anthropologists to signs in which the number of limbs in a human figure are multiplied. Such a surplus of arms or legs was common in Neolithic cultures and a recent discovery has shown them to be a feature of the Paleolithic period as well (figs. 18*a* and *b*). Some traditional types of kilim, containing figures like the ones in drawing 18*a*, very similar to the ones in the following drawing, lead one to reflect on the striking survival of Neolithic symbology in carpets that are only three hundred years old at the most. In kilims the hyperanthropic motifs of the goddess's arms alter her appearance to the point where she is transformed into a geometric figure, such as a rhombus or hexagon (fig. 8). We see, in this case, the small *wrench-shaped* head with two curved arms that are repeated six times in each body; under this hyperanthropic development, it is possible to recognize the legs in the two spirals that curve in the opposite direction to those of the arms. The same motif recurs in the three concentric representations of the goddess and, in a mirror image, in the symmetrical part of the kilim, creating a hexagon that is repeated three times. In figure 19 the hyperanthropic motif of the arms is repeated four times

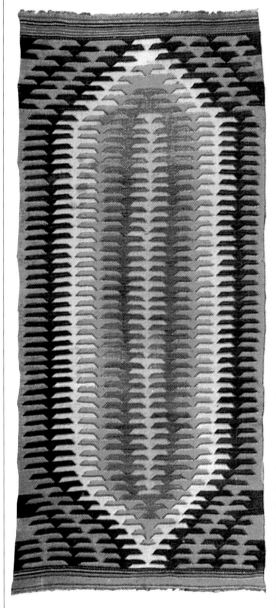

19. Kilim with hyperanthropic pattern.

in a concentric pattern so as to create a single elongated hexagon.

The result (we can never know if it was also the objective) is a geometric pattern underlined by spiral motifs in which the anthropomorphic goddess is concealed and appears only at a second level of observation. In this way, in my opinion, the symbols subtending the representation cancel each other out but are superimposed, allowing us to speak not only of the significance of the body of the goddess, but also of the meaning of the spiral, the hexagon and the hyperanthropic motif.

Although I will have occasion to go back to the geometric patterns further on, it is perhaps worth saying a few words about hyperanthropomorphism at this point, even if its symbolic meaning is now well known and basically accepted.

The multiplication of limbs reflects the desire to emphasize what they represented in the life of the remote past: strength, speed, control over movements, the creative capacity, skill in hunting, endurance in running, and so on. So it is an unconscious expression, through *concrete* signs, of an *abstract* dimension of the depicted personality, to which is attributed a value not recognizable in the body (the same as all the others) but revealed by means of the emphasis provided by multiplication. When the hyperanthropic character refers to the Mother Goddess, we can only see it as a sign of a power so vast and deep as to get lost in the space, losing its original distinctive features to blend with the totality of the universe in a form that recalls the cosmic egg or the mandala, the original nucleus in which matter and energy were fused.

[1] The fate chosen by Saint Agnes according to the Christian legend.
[2] The natural dyes used in kilims are made out of mineral, animal, and vegetable elements.
[3] J. Mellaart, *The Goddess from Anatolia*, Eskenazi, Milan 1989, p. 56.

The Primordial Water

"The Ocean father of all things," declared the ancient philosopher of nature Thales, as did Homer and, before them, so many cosmogonic myths from all over the world, from Spain to Polynesia, recalling that "in the beginning there was only a great expanse of water, immersed in darkness." "All was water," we are told by the Indian texts. "The great waters met no shores," states a Taoist text. According to the Chinese water is the *wou-ki*, the original chaos, the indistinct, that which exists prior to any separation, and therefore prior to any form of life or consciousness.

The reference to a watery and dark infinity is symbolically linked to the amniotic fluid, to gestation in the darkness of the womb, but the element water, which takes the form of whatever contains it, also represents the infinite variety of the possible, "all the virtual, the formless, the germ of germs, all the promises of growth, but all the risks of regression as well,"[1] and in this sense the analogies among water, the mother and the unconscious are truly striking. The densely symbolic content of a Vedic prayer tells us what can be requested from the primordial waters. "O you rich waters / that reign over opulence / and preserve favorable destiny and immortality; / you that are sovereigns of wealth / companions of good posterity / deign Sarasvati to grant this youthful vigor / to he who sings."[2] But the association of water with the raw material, the fertility and the origin of everything is only one part of the archetypal dimension of this element. Water is ambivalent because it is at once heavenly and earthly, beneficent and destructive, just like the bull and the moon. Rain, dew and snow fall from the sky, bringing balm to the earth and making it fertile, and, as a penetrative element, belong to the realm of masculine symbology. Rivers, springs, lakes, seas and marshes, on the other hand, are the waters of the earth that, like pots, contain life. They are therefore assigned to the world of feminine archetypes.

A Babylonian cosmogonic myth recounts that, before creation, there was neither heaven nor earth but that the primordial waters had extended everywhere and always.

The second aspect of the ambivalence of water concerns its simultaneously beneficent and destructive nature: for the peoples of remote antiquity in particular, who did not know how to conserve it, water was a daily matter of life and death. On the one hand deluges, storms and floods; on the other springs, hoarfrost, the calm waves of a lake. Faced with such ambivalence how could they avoid contradictory feelings of fear and love? The same contradictory feelings that they had toward the bull and the Mother Goddess. In Anatolia, as in other temperate regions of Asia Minor, water constituted the precious asset that was the cause and origin of the first civilizations. The Tigris, Euphrates and Nile had permitted the development of the Mesopotamian and Egyptian cultures. But in the Neolithic period, as James Mellaart has pointed

20. Mesopotamian sculpture from the third millennium BC.

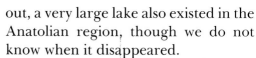

out, a very large lake also existed in the Anatolian region, though we do not know when it disappeared.

The cult of water was handed down with particular insistence by all the civilizations of the Middle Eastern basin. The Mesopotamian sculpture from the 3rd millennium BC in figure 20, for example, represents a goddess holding a pot from which water gushes in two directions. Fish can be seen in the water. Water emerges from the earth (the pot) and life flows in it. The image is no different, in its meaning, from the one in the fresco from Çatal Hüyük reproduced in figure 21. Here, in the third "niche" from left, we can see water[3] flowing from the nostrils of the bull in two opposite directions. The bull, like the pot, is an image identified with the archety-

pal combination earth- mother-nature. In figure 22 we see water spouting from the belly of the goddess and flowing in a double pair of directions, up and down, left and right. In figure 7 the same images can be found again, with different associations: the row of bull's heads at the edges of the painting enclose triangles with the point downward, a symbol of the female sex. The large symbolic belly of the goddess contain life: three drops of water, perhaps three eggs. More water flows from the hands of the divinity, in the form of drops with small fish swimming in them.

In the kilims we find all these symbols of water again, always represented in blue, emerging from the maternal womb: in figure 23 it is possible to detect an interesting analogy with the

frescoes in figure 22, where the water flows in waves in two directions, gushing from the maternal womb in a flow that underlines the character of fertility. This liquid (a word connected with the Latin *linquere*, a term of Indo-European origin that means *to leave* or *let go*) is in fact allowed to flow from the goddess in a continuous stream that starts from the vital center of her own being, from the biological center of creation.

[1] Var. Authors, *Dictionnaire des symboles*, Seghers, Paris 1980, vol. II, p. 221.
[2] "Asvalayana Strantasutra" 4.13, in *Le Veda*, Gallimard, Paris, p. 270.
[3] It is possible, as we shall see further on, to regard the liquid that emerges from the bull's nostrils as blood; in this case the symbol requires a different interpretation.

The Open Hands

On some of the frescoed walls at Çatal Hüyük can be seen rows of hands with their palms open and their fingers stretched upwards, as if they were handprints (fig. 24).

We can find hands with the same characteristics, although highly stylized, in various types of kilim and, as is common in iconography up until the third millennium, they only have three fingers. In figure 25, the three-fingered hands extend horizontally from a hexagon containing the double-headed axe. In figure 26 the hands are stretched vertically as far as the sides of the lozenge-shaped designs, which represent the double triangle.

We can see other hands, connected with the cult of the Mother Goddess, in figures 27, 28 and 29. These anthropomorphic representations attest to the symbolic value and significance of hands: in the first image the hands emphasize the form of the belly as a vessel, in the second they *hold* a baby at the breast, and in the third they are raised in prayer, as they probably are in the painting at Çatal Hüyük. In each of these cases the hands describe an activity that has, as it always does in the oldest cultures, a sacred value linked to the process of gaining knowledge. Just as children explore by touching things, in the remote past human beings attained knowledge partly through touch, by taking hold of things, pointing them out, feeling the difference: this is warm, that is damp; this is soft, that is rough.... Experimentation is also a hands-on activity and knowledge is above all experimentation. It follows that the hand, inevitably, builds, destroys, seizes and holds, proposing the principle of the original duality once again in the succession of these actions. In ancient times the hand was also used to express possession and power, drawing something toward itself and taking hold of it, just as we see small children do before they have learned to speak. It is for this reason, I believe, that in ancient Hebrew the word *iad* meant both *hand* and *power*.

If the hand is all this, if the hand shows, reaches out, knows, prays, builds, destroys, and conquers, then we may conclude that it is above all a manifestation of personal identity and, when the

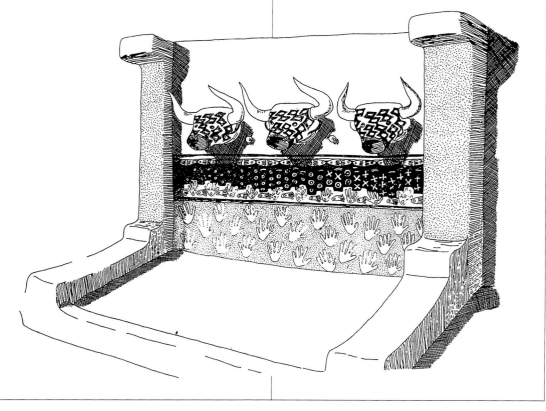

24. Çatal Hüyük.
Reconstruction of the wall
of a shrine.

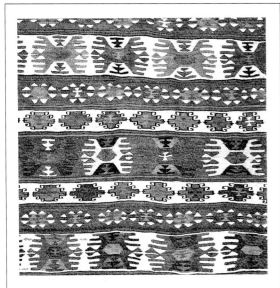

25. Detail of kilim cat. 55.

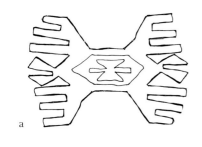

a

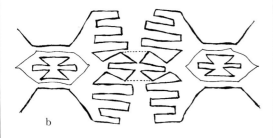

b

25a. Image of outstretched hands taken from the kilim reproduced above.
25b. The symmetrical opposition of the two goddess's heads creates the double-headed axe in negative.

26. Kilim with stylization of outstretched three-fingered hands (cat. 14).

hands are many, of collective identity. In this case the implicit statement that is being made in the kilims and in the Neolithic frescoes might be: "We are here, we know that we are here. Our hands are the representation of our ability to act on matter, to transform it and to express our personality in decision, in possession, in command and in worship."

In the kilim reproduced in figure 26 the dominant anthropomorphic theme of the hands is interwoven with the numerical theme of seven. There are in fact seven colors and seven hands in the largest figures in each of the symmetrical halves, seven *cavities* in the geometric pattern (in both the upward and the downward direction), and finally seven parts that make up the central image, since the two upper niches and the two lower ones are joined together by the seam to form a center.

In all cultures seven is the symbol of spatiotemporal totality, the conclusion of a work or the completion of a cycle: seven are the days of Biblical creation, seven the branches of the cosmic tree, seven the Hesperides, the doors of Thebes, the emblems of Buddha and the circuits around Mecca. However the key to the mystery of the symbol is not to be found in the Neolithic period since all these images date from much later than those of the fragments from Çatal Hüyük, from which they derive and whose meaning they supplement and render more complex. What did it

mean, to draw the symbol of seven, nine thousand years ago? Observation of nature tells us that each phase of the moon lasts seven days and the entire cycle twenty-eight days, and we know that the lunar month was one of the first natural phenomena to be calculated numerically. Other cycles, such as the female menstrual cycle, correspond to the phases of the moon with a constancy that must have attracted attention very early in the course of evolution. If, on the other hand, the menstrual cycle was connected with fertility, it is likely that fertility was symbolically connected to the moon and to the numbers seven and four. In fact the kilim in figure 26 is not only subdivided into seven sections, but four of these have a white ground. We can also see, in the same kilim, an example of the principle of *reductio ad unum*, i.e. the attainment of unity, the carrying of the work to its conclusion. Seven (the hands) is linked to four (the white spaces on which, in representation of the cyclic time of creation, they are woven). Seven is again linked with two (the brown spaces), symbol of the duality in the creative principle, and finally with one (the central green space). Here, in my opinion, green represents the synthesis of a totality, the *reductio ad unum* to be precise, that is translated into the eternity of a single life cycle.

If we then add up the total number of hands in this kilim we get "the number forty-nine which, as the square of sev-

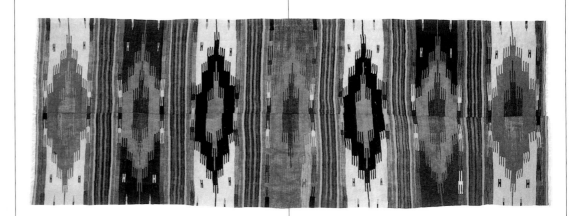

27. *Figure of the goddess with her hands on her belly. France, fifth millennium BC.*

28. *Figure of nursing goddess. Serbia, fifth millennium BC.*

29. *Figure of the Great Goddess with hands outstretched. Crete, 1300 BC.*

en, has the same cyclical meaning for the Tibetan Buddhists as the number forty has for the Jews, Christians and Muslims,"[1] that is to say the number of days required for the dead person to reach his or her final home: in this case the completion of the cycle is the completion of the human journey.

Fertility means to give birth and therefore to give rise to an independent and *total* being, destined to follow its own cycle of life. So to give birth also means to conclude an *opus*, to bring a cycle to a close and, *for this very reason*, to set another one going at the same time.

So we can imagine that in ancient cultures the repetition of an action, a word, or a design seven times must have been a sacred operation. Traces of this survive in the recurrence of the number seven in folk tales (the seven dwarfs, the seven-league boots, the wearing out of seven pairs of shoes and so on) and in superstitions that are to be found in many parts of the world. Even today in Morocco, for instance, sterile women still sometimes wrap their belts seven times around the trunk of certain kinds of trees and then secure it to one of seven ropes attached to the tree.[2]

At the moment of birth, in Iran, a lamp is lit and placed on a tablecloth decorated with seven kinds of fruit and seven types of herb.[3] So if, as seems highly likely, seven was a sacred number, the link between this numerical theme and the theme of the raised hands, probably in a gesture of prayer, would indicate, according to my hypothesis, a request for fertility for women and the earth, addressed to the goddess through the invocation of the hands and the repetition of the ritual number.

[1] Var. Authors, *Dictionnaire des symboles*, Seghers, Paris 1980, vol. II, p. 267.
[2] E. Westermerck, *Ritual and Belief in Morocco*, London 1926.
[3] H. Masse, *Croyances et coutumes persanes*, Paris 1938.

The Double-Headed Axe

The double-headed axe, an extremely ancient image recurrent in the cultures of Asia Minor, Crete, North Africa, North America, Greece and even China, has a shape similar to a butterfly: two triangles set symmetrically on the sides of a segment.

This image is also to be found in the paintings at Çatal Hüyük. In figure 45 we can see the axe in black on a ground with black dots; in figure 31 we see it, again in black, in the shape of the robe (undoubtedly used for the funeral rites) worn by the human figure at bottom right. In this case the image as a whole depicts the funerary custom (still in use in the modern era in the Zoroastrian religion) of the ancient Anatolian town, which involved exposing the corpses to vultures to strip the skeleton of flesh before burial. In figure 30 we can see other images of the double-headed axe. The black costume in the shape of a double-headed axe painted many times on an Attic crater (fig. 32) dates from 750 BC (six thousand years later), and once again the images refer to funeral rites. In kilims the form of the double-headed axe, though very common, is rarely the dominant motif (fig. 33). I think it worth pointing out, however, that the same image is often concealed in the negative of another design (fig. 25). In every band of this kilim the two stylized heads of the goddess, projected outward, meet to form the image of the double-headed axe in negative, as if to signify that the goddess is looking at or considering the duality of life and death implicit in the symbolic meaning of this primordial sacred implement.

In figure 34, which is based on a Phrygian kilim of the seventh century of our own era, the weaving of the double-headed axe in positive and negative constitutes the dominant theme of the entire composition.

Another peculiarity in the weaving of the double-headed axe is the frequent

30. Çatal Hüyük. Reconstruction of wall painting with images of double-headed axes.

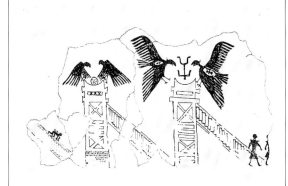

31. Çatal Hüyük. Reconstruction of wall painting with figure in funeral dress.

32. Funeral crater from the eighth century BC with figures whose clothing forms double-headed axes. Athens, National Museum.

emphatic multiplication of the form (fig. 35): the double-headed axe, the initial nucleus in the center of the design, expands *in waves*, repeating itself and growing larger until it loses, apparently, its original shape. This hypertrophic iconographic manifestation takes on, in my view, the same symbolic value as the hyperanthropic forms, that of giving a particular intensity of stress to the image represented.

I have already discussed the dual value of the double-headed axe, with particular reference to life and death. We know that it was an image sacred to the Mother Goddess and, as in the oldest North African religions, was an attribute of priestesses. Yet it is possible to formulate another hypothesis: that it was also one of the first implements made by human beings, first out of stone, then flint, and finally metal. "The stone axe," writes André Virel "was the first human weapon cum tool [...] that could penetrate, open up the material world [...] and therefore represents its complementary inseparability. The axe is a center of integration,

the expression of a permanence, an accumulated flash of lightning."[1]

Earth exists. The axe is a human creation capable of breaking the earth: so we really are dealing with an indissociable complementarity here, in which the raw material is united with (perhaps) the first product of culture. This is why, in my view, at Çatal Hüyük (figs. 9 and 21), in the Cretan culture (inside the underground passages of the Knossos palace) and in kilims (fig. 35), the theme of the double-headed axe is so often associated with that of the cave, the niche, the underground passage that is excavated with the strength of the body and the mind. In this context the double-headed axe is not only a symbol of the duality life/death but also the primordial image of the specifically human capacity to distinguish and separate. It represents the transforming effect of consciousness on reality and therefore the reflective attitude necessary to all individual creation.

[1] Var. Authors, *Dictionnaire des symboles*, Seghers, Paris 1980, vol. III, p. 10.

33. Kilim with images of double-headed axes (cat. 121).

34. Detail of Phrygian kilim from the seventh century AD with double-headed axes.

35. Detail of kilim with hypertrophic motif of the double-headed axe.

36. Details of kilim with hypertrophic motif of the double-headed axe inside a stylized cave (cats. 133 and 139).

The Six-Pointed Star	Hacilar is a late Neolithic settlement located three hundred kilometers from Çatal Hüyük. The two towns were destroyed at more or less the same time, around 6000 BC. James Mellaart, who directed the excavations at Hacilar for four years, has written that the main innovation of that culture with respect to Çatal Hüyük was the development of painted pottery. And it is on a pot from Hacilar (fig. 37) that the design of a particular form of star (known in fact as the star of Hacilar) was found for the first time: a motif that has systematically appeared in kilims down to the present day (figs. 38, 39).

During further excavations carried out at Çatal Hüyük the same star was found in wall paintings. It can be seen in figure 45, where it is recognizable in the fragments of the upper border.

The star of Hacilar is made up of three symmetrical double triangles, as is shown in figure 42. This composition gives rise to a star shape subdivided into six triangles that circumscribe a rhombus (the same rhombus as is visible in figure 37, painted on the other side of the vase as well). In kilims the star of Hacilar always has a symbol of duality in the middle. When this is not a rhombus, it is a double triangle (fig. 39). Sometimes the rhombus is in two colors (two interlocking horns), as in figures 40 and 41 (which are reminiscent of the symbol of yin and yang).

Only in one situation have I come across the consistent absence of the dual symbol at the center of the star, and that is when this symbol is located at the meeting point of the two symmetrical parts of the kilim, that is where the central rhombus is cut in two by the seam (cat. 63). In any case the central rhombus does not need to be depicted in two colors in order to express the *one* through the *two*, for unity is manifest through the two parts of the kilim itself. In kilims sometimes only the upper (or lower) half of the star of Hacilar is rep-

resented, but in such cases, as is shown in figure 42, the image is colored differently so as to draw attention to the three negative triangles as well as the positive ones, thereby recreating the geometric shape of the hexagon. Both the shape of the double triangle (figs. 44a, b) and the star of David, or seal of Solomon (fig. 43a), are common in the weaving of kilims. If we examine these two figures we see how the two triangles, which in the first drawing touch at one point and are arranged symmetrically with respect to it, are superimposed in the second, giving rise to the characteristic six points. If we now compare the star of David with the star of Hacilar, we can see how the pairs of triangles in figure 42 are reversed in figure 43, so that their vertices point outward: in this way the center of the star of Hacilar forms a rhombus and the center of the star of David becomes a hexagon, while the two double-headed axes at the side remain the same.

What does this signify? What meaning does the star have on the pots from Hacilar and the walls at Çatal Hüyük,[1] and both stars on kilims of every age?

I am inclined to think that the chief meaning of these stars lies in the repetition of the number six (the double triangles) which gives rise to the number seven (represented by the center). I have already discussed the number seven in this book, but I would like to remind the reader here of its significance of centrality, of cosmic totality, of the conclusion of a work or a cycle that, in itself, clears the way for another work or another cycle. The two stars serve to indicate an image of dynamic totality that extends to infinity.

From the development of the double-headed axe and the double triangle—two images of which one is the negative of the other (fig. 44)—arise two forms in which duality is contained and, at the same time, superseded by the idea of totality and infinity expressed by the

37. Terracotta from Hacilar.

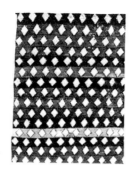

38. 39. Details of two kilims, one with six-pointed stars containing a rhombus, the other with a continuous pattern of rhombuses.

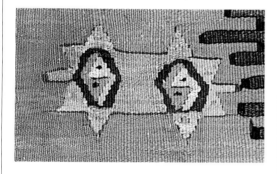

40. 41. Details of kilims (cats. 13 and 79) that recall the image of yin and yáng.

42a. Star of Hacilar.
42b. Half star of Hacilar that is completed by including the parts in negative.

star. All these meanings, worked out on a conscious level through analysis of these figures, were already contained *in nuce* in the unconscious of the Aeneolithic peoples of Anatolia, as I have tried to show at the beginning of this book. The universe of symbols was already structured into images, right from the outset, in the human psyche: over the course of time they emerged and over the course of time they were understood, but they were already there. So it was the idea of the Cosmos that the two stars expressed: Cosmos, the organizing principle, the structuring of matter and energy, in contrast to Chaos, that which was there before the big bang and which found form and meaning afterward.

The Cosmos constitutes the archetypal model that is followed by the human race in its actions, steering matter and energy in the direction required by its plans. The quest for the absolute, perfection and totality is an irrepressible impulse of the human psyche, even if it is destined for perpetual frustration, and one that is archetypically manifest in the idea of perfection and completeness of form and graphically expressed in the two stars.

Cosmogony, said Mircea Eliade, is the exemplary model for any *action*: not only because the Cosmos is the ideal archetype of every creative situation, but also because the Cosmos, a divine work, is hallowed in its very structure. By extension, everything that is perfect, full, harmonious and fertile, in other words everything that is cosmic, everything that resembles a Cosmos, is sacred.

To do something well, to work, build, structure, shape, mold, form, all this signifies generating life and molding it, and in the last instance making it resemble the harmonious organism *par excellence*, the Cosmos. And the Cosmos, let us repeat, is the exemplary work of the gods, their masterpiece.

By tracing the star of Hacilar or the star of David, then, one gives form to the idea of completed work, of concluded cycle, or of ordered and harmonious totality, and therefore of completion and perfection.

So far we have stressed the common aspect of the two stars but, as we have seen, they are different, and I believe that it is in the inversion of the two triangles—in the star of Hacilar their vertices point inward, in the star of David they point outward—that we have to look for the symbolic meaning of this difference. In the first case, in fact, the energy seems to implode, in the second to explode, as if to indicate the phases of contraction and expansion that govern the circuit of matter/energy. They are the inhalation and exhalation of the Cosmos; the nothing and the all. According to an Indian cosmogonic myth, the world is created when Shiva breathes out and returns to the void when he breathes in, in a cosmic cycle of the universe that echoes the biolog-

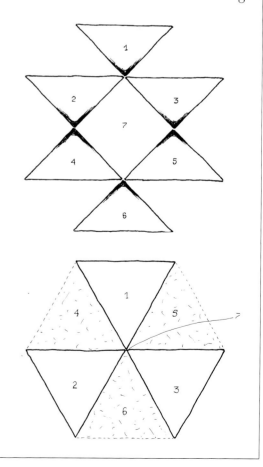

43. Detail of kilim with stars
of David (cat. 63).

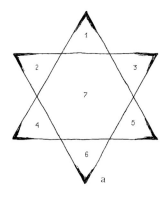

43a. Star of David or seal
of Solomon.

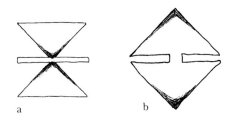

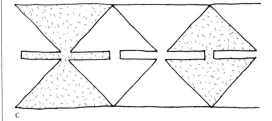

44a. b. Double-headed axe
and negative of the same
motif.
44c. Motif of combined
double-headed axes in
positive and negative.

ical one of humanity. Human beings come *out* of the mother's womb and are thrust into life, charged with explosive and extroverted energy. Then in the second half of their life, develop an introverted and implosive energy until, at the end, they go back into the earth, into the nothing from which they had come and from which they will return in another form, in another cycle. But the star of David gives rise to a number of other reflections that are based on the ancient discipline known as gematria. Gematria is a method of interpreting sacred texts on the basis of the numerical value of the letters of each word, made possible by the fact that, in the Hebrew and Greek tongues, letters are also numbers.

In ancient Hebrew, for example, the term "this world" corresponds to the number 163 and the term "future world" corresponds to the number 154. So the numerical difference between the two expressions is nine. But nine is half of eighteen and eighteen corresponds to the word *hai*, or life.

This example allows me to formulate a hypothesis for interpretation of the most common of the "magic squares" that have been known in the Islamic world ever since the tenth century.

4	9	2
3	5	7
8	1	6

This arrangement of numbers achieves a magical equilibrium because it contains all the numbers from one to nine and because, when the three numbers in each column are added up vertically or horizontally, the same result is obtained. In this case the Islamic tradition holds that two pieces of cloth with this arrangement of numbers on them should be placed under the feet of a woman when she is about to give birth,

in order to propitiate the event. And for what other reason than that it is good for a child to enter into symbolic contact with the world through the numbers that represent it?

Following an analogous procedure, we can use the same magic square to derive seven from the union of the numbers, through a line that joins the one, two and three, forming a triangle, and then joining the four, five and six in the same way, and finally the seven, eight and nine. The pattern produced by these lines is a double, intersecting and superimposed triangle: the six-pointed star of David (whose vertices are the three, nine, two, seven and eight), as can be seen in the following diagram.

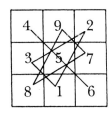

Thus we can see that, even starting out from the magic square, seven assumes an extraordinary significance in the design of the star of David, for the double intersecting triangle gives rise to six points, to which is added, as the seventh element, a hexagonal center.

The line of intersection, linking the four to the six, is the one of such singular value that serves to indicate, in the separation of the design into two, the fundamental duality of every unitary manifestation of life.

So, in the multiplicity of its forms, the kilim seems to anticipate a synthesis of a set of fundamental values that were to find expression over the course of time in the ancient cultures of the Mediterranean.

[1] I would venture to suggest that, if we were to continue excavating Neolithic sites in Anatolia, we would find the design of the star of David, which, in the present state of knowledge, pertains to a culture dating from over three thousand years later.

The Cave

A Turkish legend from the fourteenth century tells us how one day, on the Black Mountain located on the borders of China, a cave had been flooded. The water brought mud with it and, little by little, had filled up a pit shaped like a human being. In this way the pit became a sort of impression of a body. Nine months went by and, through the heat of the sun, the shape made out of mud came to life: the first man was born and he was called Ay-Atam, Father Moon. For forty years he lived by himself, and then a new flood filled the pit again and after nine months another human being was born. This time, however, the baking was incomplete, and what came out was a woman.[1] From their union forty children were born who in turn married one another and produced other children... until one day the progenitors died and, in the hope of restoring them to life, the eldest son buried them both in the pit inside the cave from which they had been born.[2]

I find the wealth of the symbolic contents of this myth and the precision with which it describes the archetypal idea of the cave extraordinary.

The event takes place in China, on the Black Mountain, in a dark place at the limits of the world (to the East): this introduction seems to indicate that the whole story springs from unconscious impulses. In the first episode the allegory of birth is transparent: the cave represents the symbolic place where the human being takes shape, comes to life, is born and then returns when life comes to an end, perhaps to be born a second time. The cave is the earth that, soaked with water and heated by the sun, gives birth to the ear of grain, whose seed again falls to earth to decompose and give rise, in the mystery of darkness, to the new shoot.

The cave is a dark and mysterious place because it is not possible to see the conception of life, only to ascertain that it has occurred. For this reason the cave, like the earth and like the mother's womb, has been symbolically perceived by many ancient cultures as an extraordinary center of chthonic energies. It suffices to think of the spirals, the double images of energy painted or carved innumerable times in caves (fig. 45) and on the bellies of Mother Goddesses (fig. 15). Cybele was also considered a divinity of caves, and the labyrinth was originally a special cave, sacred to the cult of Ariadne, the ancient pre-Helladic goddess of Crete. The cave served as a reminder of the dark and mysterious place where the continual transformation of matter and energy occurs, the symbolic location of the hope for a new life that the legend was intended to affirm in the face of the inevitability of death. Over the course of time it became the preferred location for initiation rites that promised the adept birth into a new life. For the same reason, a cave was almost always the starting point for the descent into the nether world, into the subterranean darkness where the mystery of rebirth took place.

Innumerable religions and myths testify to the meaning of this image. The central core of the Eleusinian mysteries, the most ancient initiation rite linked to the cycle of eternal recurrence, took place inside a cave. In the *taurobolium*, which has already been described in this book, the initiation was carried out in a pit. Jesus, the promise of eternal life, was born in a grotto.

Just as in the religious iconography of every age, the theme of the cave is recurrent in the frescoes of Çatal Hüyük and in kilims, as is clear from the numerous pictures of kilims reproduced in this volume.

In the light of the symbology of the cave, and in view of its frequent presence in the wall paintings and textiles, it might be conjectured that kilims were originally also intended for use in the

45. *Çatal Hüyük.*
Reconstruction of the wall
painting "of the seven caves."

cult of the dead. Support for this idea comes from the image of the tower visible on the far right of figure 45 and at the sides of each cave in figure 47, since—as I have already pointed out in connection with figure 31—these towers were altars used for the exposure of corpses to vultures prior to burial.

The *fresco of the seven caves* (fig. 45), an extraordinarily interesting piece of historical evidence from the viewpoint of the study of religious symbolism, depicts the whole course of human existence in its seven images, from an origin that already contains its end to an end that already contains a new origin.

The symbol of the Mother Goddess is present in its different manifestations, always set inside a cave.

In the first image, the goddess is represented by a set of dual symbols. On her belly we see the intersecting pattern of two double meanders. The spiral of which they are made up is the simplest way of expressing the idea of evolution from a point of origin; it is the line that ceaselessly connects the two extremities of becoming since it is the result of two opposing forces, the centripetal force that pushes inward and the centrifugal force that pushes outward.

The spiral, which is therefore an expression of emanation, extension, development, cyclic continuity and creative rotation, symbolizes the idea of the primary energy and of the cyclical character of evolution. This is why it is to be found in all early cultures, without exception.

The double spiral (from which the swastika and the labyrinth would be developed) expresses the idea of evolu-

46. *Kilim "of the three caves"*
(cat. 154).

47. *Çatal Hüyük.*
Reconstruction of wall
painting with cave motifs.

tion in the lines stretching outward and of involution in the lines leading in toward the center, thereby indicating the two directions of movement: toward life and toward death. So in the extreme concision of this symbol, the goddess of the double meanders is once again a manifestation of the divine duality of death and rebirth, which takes place inside the womb as if inside the cave and stands for the promise of life that contains, even in gestation, the destiny of death.

In the second cave we see the image of the goddess repeated three times, with one large figure and two smaller ones. We have already come across this splitting in the chapter referring to the original duality: the goddess comprises two opposites (in color as well), but in this way she also constitutes a triple deity that is the origin of the *triple goddess* of so many later religions (the three Moirai or Fates; Persephone, Demeter, Hecate; etc.). These were generally the mistresses of birth (or of childhood), of life (or of maturity) and of death (or old age). So the three phases of human life are represented in this image.

In the third cave the bull's head holds an image of the goddess between its horns, which is identical to the one in the second cave. Alongside the bull two female figures with their legs spread wide express the power and the energy of sex and fertility, while the blood that spurts from the sacrificial bull refers to the value of blood in the life cycle and to the libidinal energy connected with it. Thus the whole of this cave speaks of the vital force and of the strength of the evolutionary spiral of youth.

The fourth niche houses a steatopygous goddess seated on two motionless leopards with their heads facing in opposite directions. Alongside are two other figures of motionless animals. This image depicts the control over inert matter, over the static, heavy, telluric aspect of reality. It represents dominion over what is always repeated in the same way in accordance with a given order and so is free of conflict: the succession of the seasons, the immobility of the earth, the phases of the moon, the daily return of the sun and so on.

Everything changes, however, in the following cave where the goddess, in her androgynous manifestation, firmly grips by the neck the destructive power embodied by the vultures. As we have seen in other parts of this book, de-

struction is inevitable if the life cycle is to be maintained — "the seed is not born if the seed does not die" — but the ancients felt the need to believe that the darkness, death and destruction that nature brings with it were an emanation of the Mother Goddess and were therefore placed under her control. The vultures devoured the body of the dead and were therefore unconscious agents of transformation within an eternal cycle over which only the nature goddess could hold sway.

The sixth cavern represents the opposite of the fourth. Here the wild beasts are upright, facing one another. The standing goddess holds them by their manes. There is nothing immobile in this image: the energy is no longer turned inward, but outward; the *dynamis* of movement is born. Here the goddess is an expression of control over the conflict between opposing energies, over the difficulty of choosing and reconciling or, as a depth psychologist would put it, over the impulse toward life and the impulse toward death that are in opposition in the human being and in nature from the beginning to the end.

Let us examine, in conclusion, the last

cave, which is symbolically akin to the first. The cycle is complete and has to start again: the egg contains an embryo and is surrounded by four vaguely visceral shapes. The cave holds and protects a mystery, the same one as ever, the mystery of life and death consumed in darkness.

Comparing figures 46 and 47, we cannot help but be struck by the extraordinary resemblance between two images separated by about eight thousand four hundred years.

The representation of the cave in the kilim (fig. 46) expresses, in addition to the symbology described above, the *reductio ad unum* of a triple form, a theme recurrent in almost all religious traditions. In fact, if we imagine superimposing the two images at the side over the one in the middle, they cancel each other out, for the solids of one coincide with the voids of the other and vice versa. In this way we obtain a single cave with a definite boundary and a completely solid (or empty) interior, containing all three figures. Nor is the color (see cat. 154) irrelevant in the fusion of the three images: in the orange and the violet, which arise out of the meeting between yellow and red and between red and blue, is expressed a chromatic marriage of gods, symbol of the duality of heaven and earth. All that is born, that lives, that dies—this kilim seems to be saying—is part of a single movement that always turns back on itself. The image, what we see, is the separation; the unity is hidden and can only be seen if one knows how to see it. This, in the end, seems to me to be the ultimate meaning of every kilim.

[1] It is hardly necessary to say that the incompleteness refers to the biological sexual difference and does not imply any value judgment with respect to the female personality. It is this small *difference in baking* that makes possible the continuation of the history!
[2] L. P. Roux, "Faune et Flore sacrées dans les soiltés altaïques," in *Dictionnaire des symboles*, Seghers, Paris 1980, vol. I, p. 228.

The Triple Form

It is common for the same design to be repeated three times in kilims, in most cases with modest variations of form and size: three huts or caves (fig. 46), three goddesses, three hexagons (fig. 8) and so on. In addition the goddess is constantly flanked by two lateral images—two vultures, two axes, two watercourses, or even two indecipherable shapes—that justify the symbolic color and bring in three once again.

Starting from the presupposition that every iconographic motif in Neolithic civilization had a cult origin, and therefore a meaning not determined by chance or aesthetic aims, and bearing in mind the direct descent of kilims from the Neolithic culture of Anatolia, we cannot help but ask what this triplication signifies.

From the symbolic viewpoint three represents first of all the completion of a manifestation, the origin of a new element from the meeting of the two opposites represented by one and two. Hence it expresses a dynamic aspect of reality and defines a point of synthesis, but at the same time it provides one element for the subsequent meeting of a new pair of opposites.

The repetition of a gesture, a form, or a formula three times is therefore a propitious omen for the successful outcome of the venture, as it means that something new will be born.

In many myths and folk tales, for instance, a series of three identical acts ensures success and at the same time constitutes an indissociable whole. Going through three doors, celebrating for three nights, or winning three pomegranates means reaching a totality, completing an action, bringing an enterprise to a conclusion. The totality of three expresses a dynamic value, while the totality of two has a static significance; in other words three places the emphasis on the synthesis that derives from it.

The linking of good and evil, for example, gives rise to a mode of human behavior that in turn will produce good and evil.

A significant symbolic meaning of three is also linked to the dimension of time. The Mediterranean cultures of a matriarchal character venerated a triple goddess of which Hecate and the Moirai were the Greek epilogue. Hecate, the black goddess of old age, death and magic, of everything dark and infernal, was represented with three faces because she also contained the two earlier phases of life: youth (Kore) and maturity (Demeter): the maiden, the mother and the crone were the three faces of time, which flows in only one direction.

In pre-Greek culture the goddess was often represented with three faces, or even with three bodies with their backs to each other and looking in different directions. In the classical, and even in the Roman era, *trivia*, or places where three roads met, were dedicated to Hecate. The three phases of life appear again in the threefold figure of the Moirai. Moira means force, and three forces preside over human existence: birth, life and death.

The Greeks saw both Hecate, in her triple form, and the Moirai as predating the Olympic and patriarchal dispensation of Zeus and in some way superior to it, since he had no power to interfere in their activities.

So it is likely that in the tradition of the kilim too the repetition of three has the same meaning of conclusion of the action and of comprehension of the entire span of life.

In most cases the triple form constitutes the central motif of the kilim, immediately attracting the observer's attention because past, present and future, birth, life and death comprise a single whole in their flow, the whole set of imaginable situations and the end of every human work, as well as the beginning and end of every kilim.

Analysis of a Kilim: the "Goddess of Rhombuses"

The kilim examined here (cat. 104) appears to be completely geometrical, dominated as it is by rhombuses and spiral patterns, but looking more closely and bearing in mind the resemblance to the paintings at Çatal Hüyük, the geometry reveals its symbolic form and hidden meaning. It is clear that drawing 16a reproduces the central motif of the kilim, but the design has an obvious anthropomorphic character that is obscured by the geometrical pattern of the weaving.

Just as in the drawing, each medallion (red, blue, purple) represents the image of the goddess, with a large belly, mirrored by the figure underneath it. The symmetrical meeting of the two bodies gives rise to a series of rhombuses inscribed one inside the other.

The steatopygous form of the deity suggests the idea of the earth, fertility, and the power of nature that causes birth and death, maintaining the equilibrium of the life cycle. This dominant double image is flanked by two lateral figures, whose stylized arms and legs form four meanders. Two of these run from right to left and two from left to right: the former indicate the way from death to life, the latter from life to death. They constitute, from this point of view, a repetition of the idea of the life cycle punctuated by birth, death and the succession of the seasons. The adherence of these spiral-shaped figures to the plane on which their hands and feet rest suggests that the four meanders have equal value.

The two figures that flank the "goddess of the rhombuses" are mirror images and identical to the two figures underneath, except for one tiny, almost invisible difference: the "head-downward" images possess a phallic attribute that is missing from the "head-upward" images. As far as the significance of the twofold repetition of the images is concerned, I refer the reader to the preceding chapters. But in this kilim it is possible to identify a special symbology linked to color which is worth examining. In this case too, the symbolic context is concealed and visible only to the knowing eye: if we superimpose the two figures of the major goddess (red and blue), we obtain the central purple figure, which is the synthesis and the principal image of the entire kilim. Blue is the color of thought, abstraction, the distant world and the heavens because it is pure, cold, immaterial and deep; red is the color of passion, of the vital energy of the earth, because it is the color of blood and fire.

Purple, which represents the *reductio ad unum* of these two forces, is therefore the color of moderation, bringing together thought and action, body and spirit, wisdom and impulse. The fourteenth arcanum of the tarot, Temperance, depicts an angel holding a blue and a red pot from which pour two colorless liquids. These meet to form a fluid that is the water of life. Purple is the condensate of the continual exchange between the chthonic red of impulsive energy and the sky blue of spiritual abstraction. This is why in Christian liturgy the bishop's mantle is purple, and Jesus' clothing is purple during the Passion, for at the moment of sacrifice he unites completely within himself Man, the son of earth, whom he is trying to redeem, and the imperishable heavenly Spirit, to which he is about to return. So the purple robe symbolically unites the Father to the Son: Jesus as a member of the human race wears a red tunic and a blue cloak; stripping himself of his human nature to become one with God, he puts on the purple robe.

As can be seen from this kilim too, the meaning of colors and their meeting has an origin that is lost in the mists of time. We should not forget, for instance, that in much Renaissance iconography, the Madonna is depicted in a red dress and a blue cloak to indicate the coming together of opposites, of the male and the female. And to conclude, we shall quote the words of Sambursky: "so Goethe, in the end, arrived at a graphic representation in which the three vertices of a triangle represent the three primary colors, while the vertices of a second triangle, which intersects the first, represent the three secondary colors, green, purple and orange. Diagonally opposite each color is its complementary color."[1]

Observe now that in the place where the bodies of the "goddess of rhombuses" meet there are three small rhombuses in a horizontal line and divided internally into two different colors, separated by a short dark segment; these two colors outline the motif of the negative of the double-headed axe in negative. We have, in this case, two groups of ternary activities where three is the number of rhombuses and an expression of the totality of a completion, and two (the negative of the double-headed axe inscribed in the rhombuses) represents the union of the opposites that can give rise to the third. The kilim seems to be saying that only the union of two opposing forces permits birth of the new, represented by three, and is thereby affirming one of the most deeply rooted (conscious or unconscious) convictions of the human species since its origins, in all the cultures of every place and time.

However the rhombus has a very special meaning of its own. As the union of two triangles with their vertices pointing upward and downward, it represents not only the symmetrical image of the primordial cave, but also the union of the *male* and the *female* triangle. Out of their union is born a quadrilateral figure that can be compared in many ways to that of the cross, which has been used as an image of the totality of creation, of the idea of the universe, ever since the most remote past and in cultures that differ greatly from one another.

According to Jung, fourfoldness represents the archetypal foundation of the human psyche: in other words, the totality of conscious and unconscious psychic processes.

Once again there seems to be a surprising correspondence between the "outer" sensible world and the inner world, enclosed within the human soul, both of which can be represented by the *quaternary* image. But two more *numerical combinations* present in this kilim make clear its symbolic meaning: these are forty and seventy-two. In fact there are forty figures of minor goddesses with their curled up hands and feet on the same plane, following one another graphically in an unbroken chain and across a space that seem to evoke the idea of time. In their descriptions of the story of salvation, Biblical commentators attribute a profound symbolic significance to this number: forty hours, forty days, forty months and forty years call to mind the hours spent by Jesus in the tomb before being restored to life, the length of the flood, the duration of Jesus' preaching and the age at which both Buddha and Muhammad commenced their preaching.

The number describes the completion of a cycle that does not lead to mere repetition, but to radical change, to the transition to another level of action and life.

In funeral rites forty is the number of days necessary for the soul to free itself of the mortal remains, for it to reach its definitive home. Between the beginning of the vultures' work at Çatal Hüyük and its conclusion forty days may have passed. The image of the two pairs of vultures in figure 31, which in fact suggests the passing of time, has a dynamic as well as static aspect. Hence it represents the completion of the journey. This is the meaning that was attributed to the number forty by peoples who followed the custom of double burial, such as the Indians of Equatorial America. And the same attribution is to be found among the Altaians, where it was the tradition for a widow, on the fortieth day after the death of her husband, to pronounce the ritual formula "now I leave you," rendering her free to remarry. The fortieth day is also the one on which the purification of the *yurt*—the Caucasian tent—is carried out after the death of the person who lived in it. The practice of quarantine (from the Italian *quaranta*, forty) also arose out of this belief that the number forty represents a life cycle.

Let us see now where the number seventy-two comes in: it can be found in the series of figures that runs along the upper and lower part of the kilim, each of which represents a double (symmetrical) goddess with a small rhombus in her belly. The symbolic meaning of seventy-two is frequently encountered in the Islamic tradition. To take just one example, there is a celebrated *hadith* holding that the prophet Muhammad once declared: "After me my community will split into seventy-three sects, of which seventy-two will perish and one will be saved."

Moving on finally to an examination of the kilim's border as a whole, we can see an unusual asymmetry in the light-colored ground of half of one of the short sides.

I like to picture this asymmetry of the border as a "way of escape," a breakthrough of the knowable and known universe into what is still invisible, ineffable and indefinable: a sort of open door onto the infinity that lies outside and inside us.

[1] S. Sambursky, "La luce e il colore nelle scienze fisiche e nella teoria goethiana," in *Il sentimento del colore*, Red Edizioni, Como 1990.

The Kilim of the Seven Goddesses

The iconography of this kilim (cat. 134) contains a series of symbols characteristic of ancient Anatolian weaving. In the central part, in fact, we can see two rows of stylized anthropomorphic images, symmetrical with one another, and set above seven swastikas. These are images related to the Mother Goddess, which represented the archetype of the union of all opposing energies in matriarchal cultures. The swastikas over which they exercise their dominion are in fact one of the oldest and most universal symbols of a dynamic principle produced by antagonistic forces.

The reference to the union of opposites can also be recognized in the choice of colors, where the opposites are represented by red and blue and their synthesis by purple (symbols of the feminine principle, the male principle and their transcendence respectively).

On the left-hand, vertical border, it is possible to make out seven symmetrical double horns; joined together they give rise to a design in negative that is known as the star of Hacilar.

On the right-hand border the double horns produce seven stars of Hacilar in positive. In all likelihood they are bull's horns, symbols of the twofold power of the maternal deity. Within the design, each star of Hacilar repeats the symbology of seven.

In addition we find that if we add up the number of bull's horns and stars of Hacilar in the two borders, we get twenty-eight, the number that represents the entire lunar cycle.

The repetition of seven, in the number of divinities, bull's horns, and stars of Hacilar, is another feature of interest in this kilim, as in numerous others. In almost all religious traditions, in fact, the number seven suggests the idea of totality.

From the whole set of these images (figures, colors and numbers) and from their combination emanates a great dynamic force that originates from the deity, is spread through the motion of the swastikas and the images of bulls, and sets the stars of Hacilar going in a symbolic movement of contraction and expansion that lies at the origin of all reality and of every manifestation of existence from the very first breath.

The Kilim of the Great Goddess

As an image begins to speak to us, we become aware that the analogies and the different messages remain linked together in any case, integral with one another like a system that always tends to grow larger. Nor is this all. The many images interact, in much the same way as words do, creating a dynamic and complex meaning that has the apparent vitality of a discourse, only to conceal itself once again behind the immobile symbols that these images have expressed.

The dominant symbols of this kilim (cat. 36) are chromatic and numerical and the images to which they refer are the body of the goddess, the vulture and the cave, in a contrast between positive and negative and between the upper and the lower part.

In fact the kilim is made up of two parts that are symmetrical, in their forms and colors, joined in the middle.

First of all let us look at the double positive-negative aspect: as far as the positive part is concerned, we see in this kilim a stylized image of the goddess, depicted three times in each of the symmetrical parts. Looking at the first and the third image (in blue and red), we can recognize a small head, two arms bent inward and two legs spread out and curved. The same design can be found in the central figure in purple and green (figs. 3 and 3a). We can also see how the three goddesses are seated above a cave with which they are symbolically connected. As far as the part in negative is concerned, it is possible to make out a goddess in the white part of the kilim (fig. 3b), repeated four times. In this case the images in positive and in negative are related to one another because the two vulture's heads—recognizable between the goddess's hands—are woven in positive, while in negative we find the two arms of the goddess that grip them. In addition it is possible to see how the bodies of the vultures and the caves coincide. The stylization of this figure is easier to recognize if it is compared with the details of frescoes at Çatal Hüyük reproduced in figs. 3c and 6a. With regard to the part in negative again, the four images of the goddess are white, fluid, elusive, partly dispersed, and indistinct against the background of the kilim, unlike the three figures of the goddess in positive that are colored, solid, precisely defined and stand out against the background of the kilim. What can all this mean? The white goddess is the "goddess of time" and her fourfold repetition links her to the phases of the lunar cycle. In addition, adding together the goddess's body and her six fingers and multiplying the sum by four, the number of times the image is repeated, we obtain twenty-eight, the number of days that make up the lunar month.

The colored goddess, on the other hand, through the chromatic *reductio ad unum*, passes from blue and red to purple and green: in other words from male and female qualities to the divine and eternal totality.

At this point it is possible to discern a symbolic interdependence between the four figures in negative and the three figures in negative: perhaps the archetype of the goddess comprises both a dynamic aspect and a static aspect, one governing the visible world and the other the invisible world, one connected with the endless flow of time and the other with nature and its life cycle.

Introduction to the Catalogue

Period

If the kilim had not been discovered for another hundred years, almost the only ones that we would have been able to examine would be the kilims produced in this century, owing to the inevitable progressive deterioration of objects that are in everyday use.

We have, however, been able to study kilims over the last twenty years and as a result it has been possible to examine kilims woven during the last century, which still preserve intact the formal and symbolic tradition of nine thousand years of history. In fact the watershed that divides the art kilim from a craft product of almost always modest pretensions was the turn of the nineteenth century. Dating kilims on one side or the other of this watershed is—in my view—a pointless undertaking.

The fact is that, prior to the twentieth century and over a period stretching back many thousands of years, the forms, designs, colors and technique of weaving kilims had always been the same. From this point of view a kilim from the sixteenth century is identical to a kilim from the nineteenth, which is in turn the same as one from the Middle Ages. This is because the most profound—religious and ritual—significance of the kilim lies in just this identical repetition, keeping faith with a tradition that assigned *those* meanings to *those* actions and *those* forms and not to other actions and other forms.

This symbolic tradition, based on rituals that have remained almost unchanged over the course of time, has been the guarantee of the longevity of the Anatolian kilim, as well as the cause of its rapid decline. In fact the introduction of synthetic chemicals to dye the yarn used for kilims at the end of the last century interrupted the continuity of this tradition, progressively and irreversibly altering the whole cycle of production: the kilim was no longer the same because it was no longer made in the same way. Thus over the space of a few decades a spell was broken that had lasted for thousands of years.

Having established, therefore, that art kilims (and therefore the ones reproduced in this book as well) were all produced prior to the twentieth century, I have not considered it necessary to date them more precisely.

Origin

Defining the origin of an old kilim is an enterprise that yields uncertain results, whether it is done in relation to the tribal group or the locality.

If—to take an example—I were to say that a kilim came from Konya or from the Otamish tribal group, I would be telling only a partial truth, and one that I believe to be without much significance, for it would also be possible for me to say that identical kilims were made before the foundation of Konya and even before the Otamish tribal group moved from Syria to Anatolia.

Moreover, even before the Oguz tribal groups (from whom the Otamish are descended) arrived in Anatolia from the northeast in the eleventh century, kilims had already been in existence, just as we know them today, for about seven thousand years.

As a consequence even identification of the locality of origin cannot be of much help, considering that the earliest kilims—looking just like the ones we know today and that we can see in these pages—are far older than the historical cities of the Middle East.

So it would not make sense—in my opinion—to distinguish the productions of the Anatolian region on the basis of characteristic differences confined to the period of the last hundred years. The only reason for doing so would be to take a historical approach, and one that is in this case reductive, given that—in all probability—these different characteristics have been interacting with one another in various ways hundreds of times over the course of the kilim's existence.

Symbolic Language

Finally I have not considered it appropriate to attempt to decipher the symbolism of each of the kilims illustrated in this volume, with the exception of a few brief comments, but have confined this undertaking—by way of example—to just a few of them. I took this decision not just and not so much to cut down on the amount of writing that had to be done, but chiefly so as to leave the reader the pleasure, once equipped with the tools, of recognizing and interpreting the symbols that have been handed down to us from an age-old culture.

The kilims that I have chosen to analyze from the symbolic viewpoint in this book are neither more beautiful nor more important than the others: the criterion for selection was the completeness and complexity of their interconnected symbols. To some extent they contain the whole heritage of archetypes that is characteristic of the world of kilims, and for this reason alone I believe that they can serve as a useful starting point and a suitable example that will help the reader to continue the work of interpreting the other reproductions on his or her own.

Only a starting point, because to understand a kilim is to make a discovery, but to make a discovery is also an act of learning, and an act of learning is always an individual undertaking.

Catalogue

The kilims presented in the catalogue (except for cat. 1 and cat. 154) belong to the private collection of Dario Valcarenghi

1
140 × 290 cm
Red kilim of "the mirrored Mother Goddess": it is possible to speculate that two people were seated at her feet, one facing the other, to discuss important matters.

2
140 × 337 cm
Six horizontal bands contain forty-two stylized hands, symbols of knowledge that enclose, within the central field, the hypertrophism of the star of Hacilar, repeated fifteen times on a red ground.

3
126 × 306 cm
Kilim representing
seventy-two double horns.

4
133 × 310 cm
This kilim presents three
hundred and thirty-three
white rhombuses on blue
and red stripes.

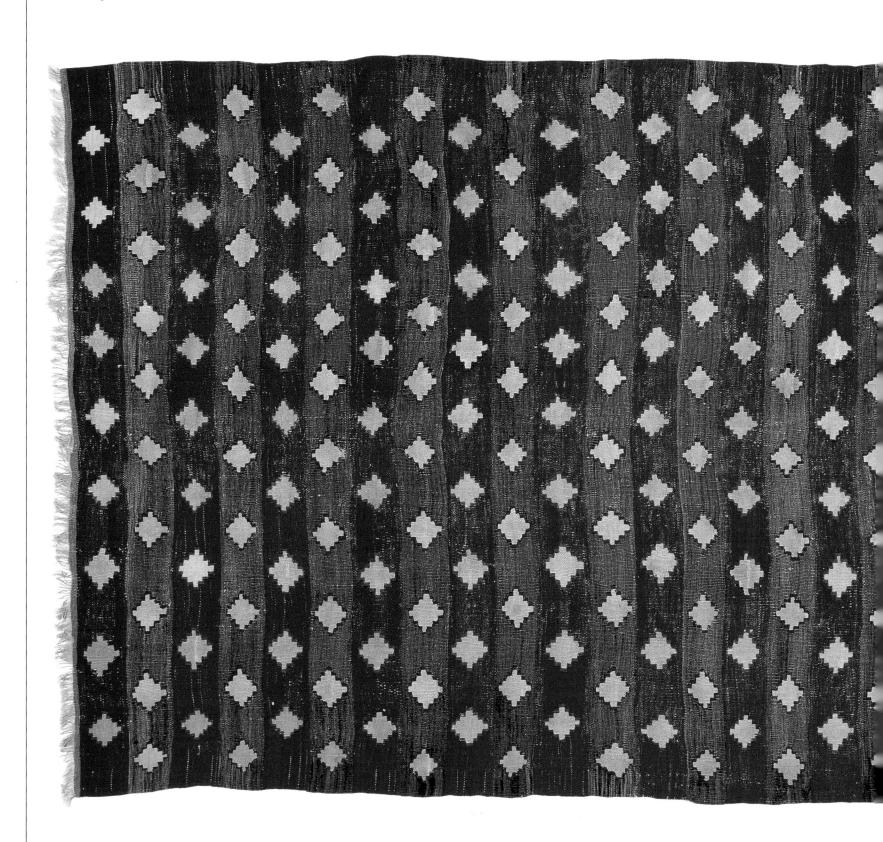

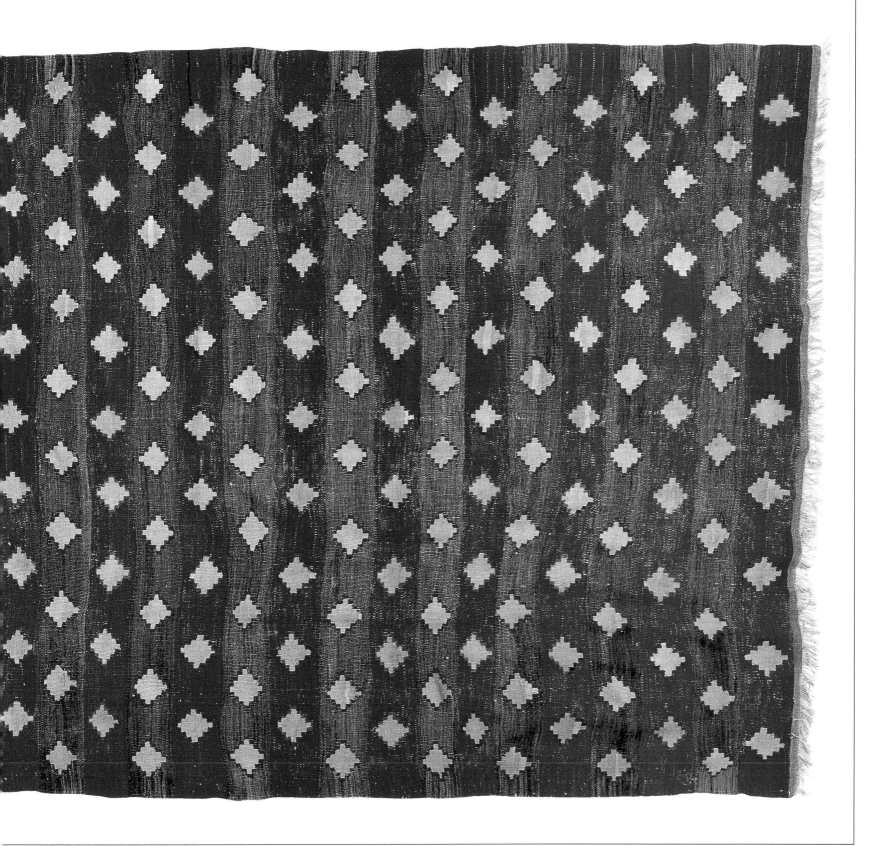

5
151 × 220 cm
This kilim bears nine
double-headed axes that
form a "magic square."

6
145 × 230 cm
In these sixteen hexagons
the figures of stars of
Hacilar are fused with two
double-headed axes with
the double triangle at the
center. The double
triangle, in turn,
represents the negative
of the double-headed axe.

7
175 × 265 cm
The rhombus that constitutes the central nucleus of the "kilim of the cave" contains a symmetrical red figure with seven fingers.

8
155 × 240 cm
It is possible that this kilim was originally made up of four bands, each containing seven double-headed axes. Thus the total number of axes would have been twenty-eight.

9
190 × 370 cm
The double figures with fingers conceal the number three in negative and the number four in positive. They interact to link up with seven and expand to take in other numerical correspondences.

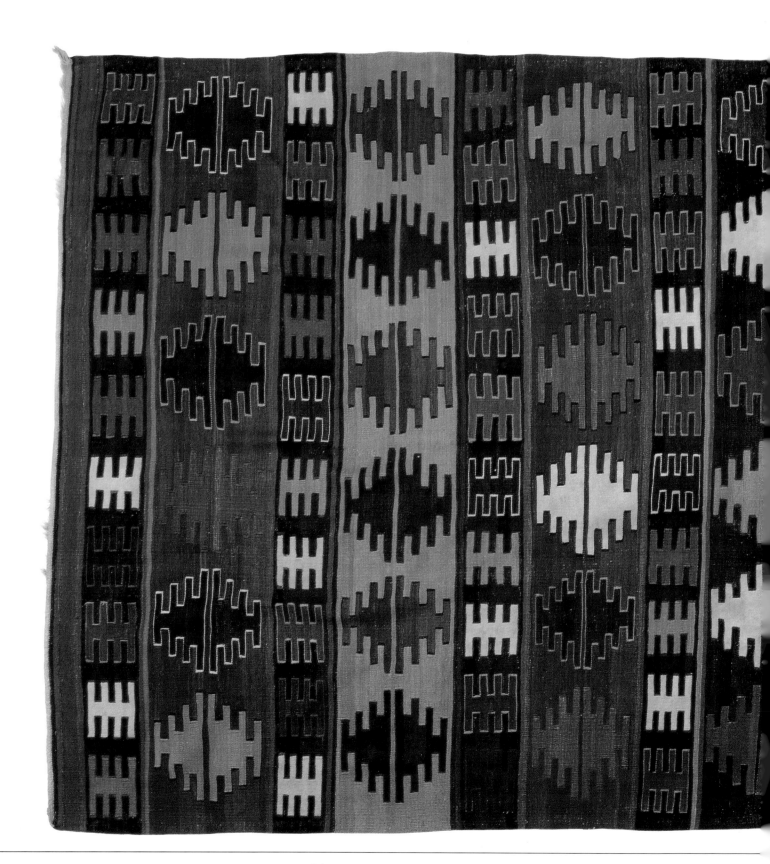

10
165 × 455 cm
The two white figures
at the sides can be split
vertically to form two
paired S-shapes, in which
a rotary movement is
discernible.

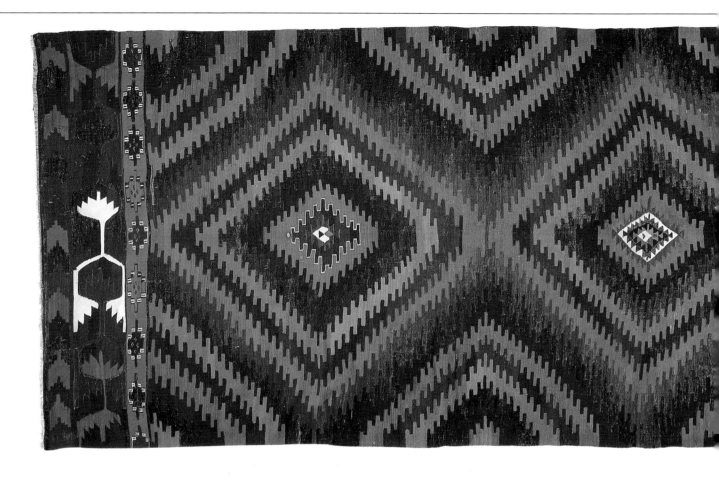

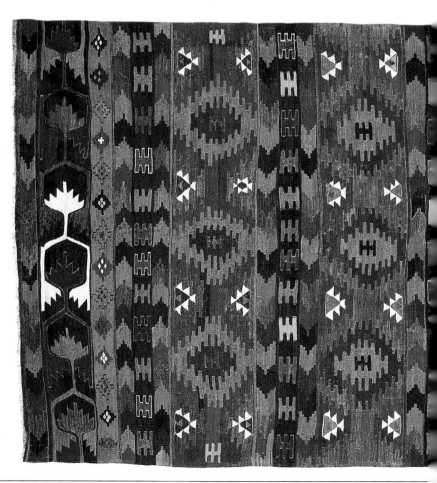

11
168 × 450 cm
At each end of the kilim
we see the white image
of the twofold goddess
of the vortex. Above and
below this figure the same
image is repeated in a
constant sequence of
colors (blue, red, white,
green, brown) that
represents the life cycle
of nature.

12
102 × 195 cm
Reading this kilim in
a horizontal direction
the image of the double
goddess, recognizable
at the ends, presents an
upward character that
is different from the
rotatory movement
of the previous kilim.

13
180 × 384 cm
In this kilim five rhombuses can be recognized, constituting five double caves.

14
141 × 390 cm
The protagonists of this
kilim are the hands of the
goddess.

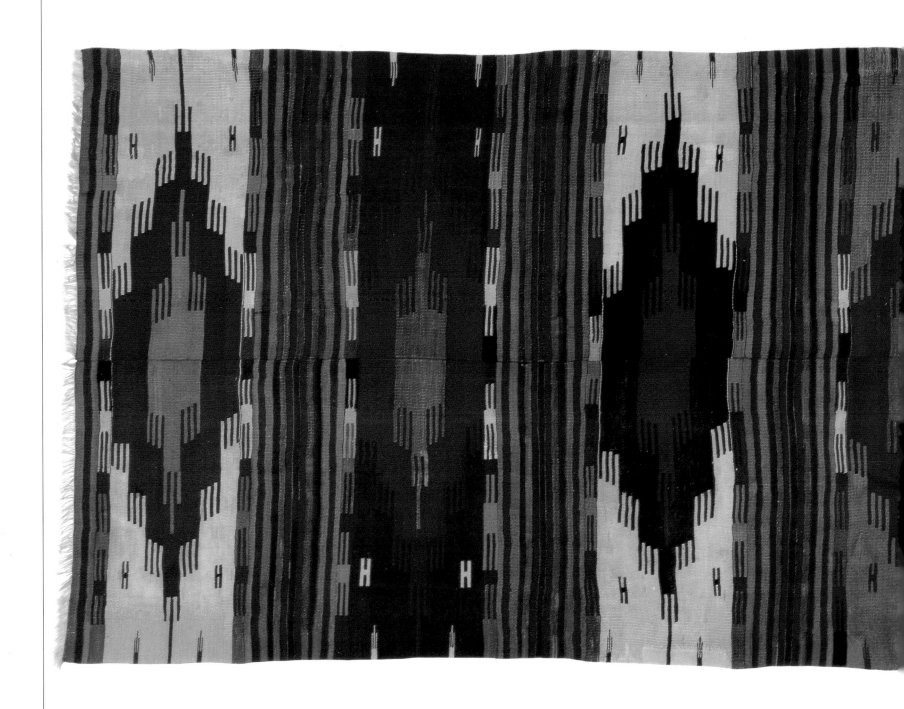

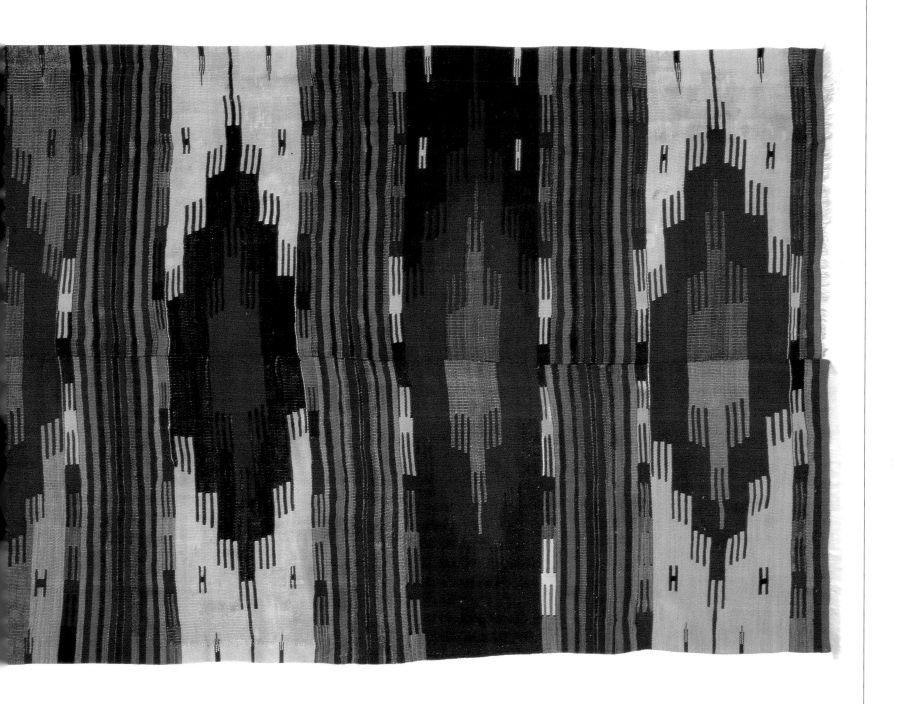

15
158 × 274 cm
Here we find the hands
again, symmetrically
joined to form seven
caves. At their point of
junction twenty-one stars
of Hacilar can be seen.

16
80 × 415 cm
In this kilim we see
a repetition of seven
in the sum of the figures
in negative and in positive
on each of its fifteen
bands.

17
180 × 390 cm
Twenty-eight double-
headed axes constitute
the characteristic feature
of this kilim and are
recognizable at the center
of each rhombus, along
with two heads of the
goddess opposite one
another.

18
154 × 418 cm
Looking at the figures
horizontally, we can see
nine mirror images of the
goddess's head, each
equipped with three
stylized fingers.

19
160 × 400 cm
In the twelve bands of this
kilim are depicted four
images, each of which
represents two vultures
facing one another.
Above the heads can be
seen the image of two
arms of the goddess
gripping the necks
of the vultures.

20
160 × 266 cm
In this kilim the central field is occupied by a series of geometrical figures that, on closer examination, turn out to be mirror images of vultures (the fringing of the feathers is visible), whose heads are depicted in negative, i.e. in white.

21
150 × 420 cm
The "ace of spades"
at the two longitudinal
extremities of each
rhombus, as in the
previous kilim, constitutes
a stylization of the
goddess gripping the
necks of two vultures,
represented in negative,
i.e. in white.

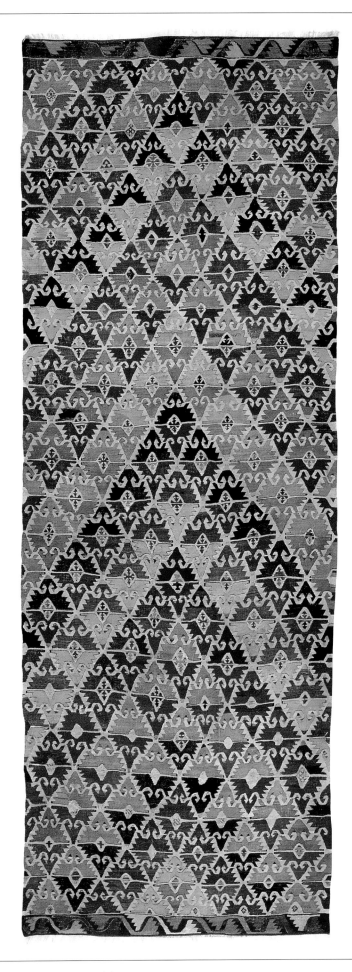

22
151 × 367 cm
In the thirty-two "cards" of this kilim some of the fundamental symbolic images in the history of the woven rug can be recognized. They include the double-headed axe, the "yin and yang" coupling, and the double head of the goddess.

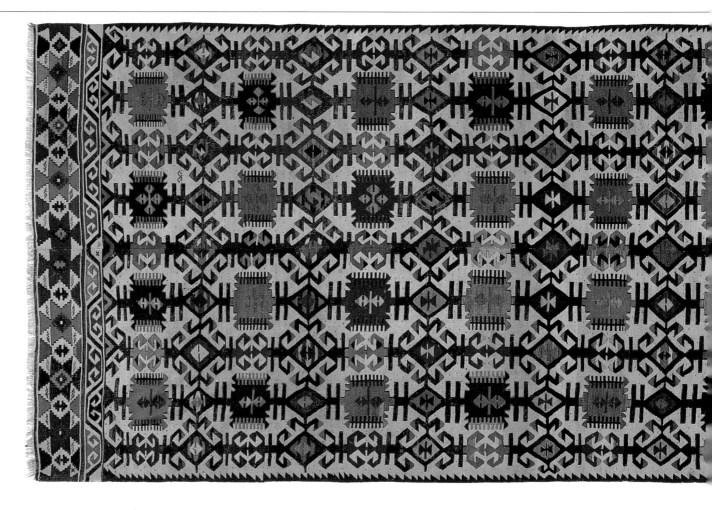

23
154 × 390 cm
On the longitudinal
borders of the rug
we see two stylized hands
that, set opposite one
another, form the image
of the double-headed axe
in negative.

24
105 × 370 cm
There are fifty figures on the four borders of the "kilim of the vultures," representing mirror images of the goddess with head and arms; at the center of the image the double-headed axe appears alternately in positive and negative.

25
120 × 374 cm
Looking at the kilim horizontally, we see in the central field, made up of two bands, the arms of the goddess set symmetrically opposite one another, both in negative and in positive. Each pair of arms, moreover, alternates in a chromatic sequence of red, blue and, finally, purple, after a series of seven figures.

26
110 × 145 cm
The twelve squares on the border are separated by patterns in the shape of an S or a tuning fork that occur frequently in the iconography of the Great Goddess.

27

174 × 410 cm
The most interesting
feature of this rug is
the chromatic sequence in
which a series of pairs in
different and symbolically
significant colors
converges on an orange-
colored center,
representing the
expansion of cosmic
energy.

28
174 × 453 cm
The unusual density of images in this kilim makes it difficult to distinguish the figures. Most of them are related to the Great Goddess, represented on the borders in mirror images, and the vulture, also in a symmetrical form, in the central field.

29
74 × 418 cm
Originally made up of two parts, this kilim has a border in which a sinuous line connects and separates the head of the goddess from the legs, which have assumed the form of roots.

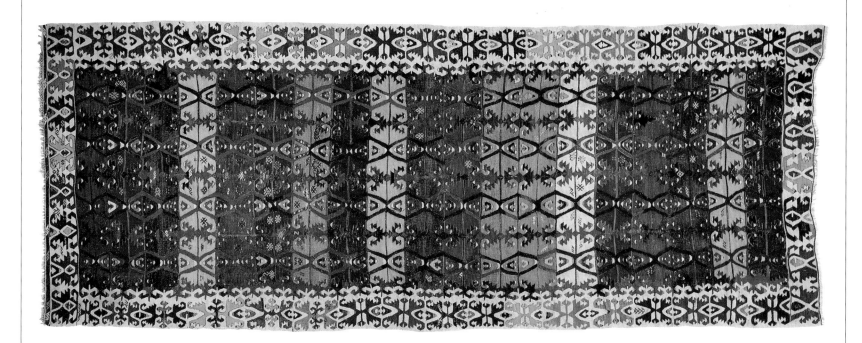

30
138 × 276 cm
In the two central
columns, on a white
ground, can be seen a
series of small double-

headed axes. They can
also be found, in an
extremely stylized and
hypertrophic form, in the
three columns on a dark
ground.

31
129 × 300 cm
On the long borders
of the rug we see
the headless body of
the goddess, represented
alternatively upright
and upside down.

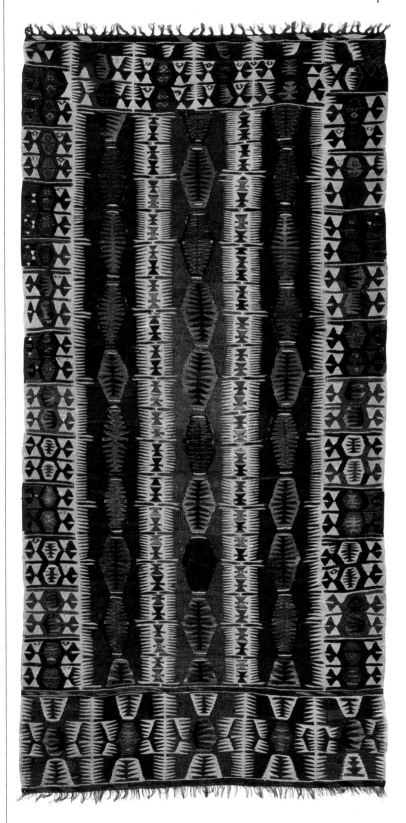

32
118 × 200 cm
The upper border contains stylized images of three-fingered hands alternating with a meandering line. In the central field the blue figures on a white ground, symmetrical and opposing, represent the goddess.

33
120 × 270 cm
In this kilim it is possible to see the double-headed axe formed in negative by the meeting of two heads of the goddess.

34
156 × 300 cm
All four borders contain
mirror images of the
goddess with her head
bowed. At the meeting
point of these symmetrical
figures we can see the
image of the double-
headed axe in negative.

35
163 × 309 cm
At the two vertical ends of this kilim we can see a series of cruciform figures, with the negative and positive images interacting to create the number twenty-eight.

156 × 368 cm
This kilim, centered
on the images of the
Great Goddess and her
attributes, is analyzed
on page 49.

37
161 × 455 cm
The borders along the
short sides of the kilim
contain the white figures
of the body of the
goddess gripping the
vultures by the neck.

38
195 × 480 cm
From the three central figures of the kilim, which we can picture as caves, extend white spirals that represent an extreme stylization of the goddess's arms.

39
92 × 390 cm
In this kilim,
distinguished by
its complex
hyperanthropism, the
themes of the cave and
the double-headed axe
are repeated.

40
150 × 400 cm
From the ends of the three central hexagons, which as we have seen are stylized images of caves, something is born, as always. In this case numerous spirals emerge that may represent the limbs of the goddess.

41

166 × 406 cm

In the two parts of the kilim located above and below the three large central "caves," we can make out nine pairs of horns set out of line; they contain S- and Z-shaped figures. In the middle of the rhombuses on the vertical borders, there are small quadrilaterals whose shape is reminiscent of the loom on which kilims are woven.

42

150 × 410 cm

A red line winds along the perimeter of the kilim, made up of many small headless figures. The border surrounds six symmetrical geometrical forms in white that seem to represent the goddess with open arms.

43
166 × 433 cm
The small, stylized head
of the goddess, located
at the upper and lower
vertex of each hexagon,
seems to be equipped with
many arms that ring the
edges of the hexagon.

44

158 × 458 cm

In this rug the chromatic sequence entails the convergence of a series of pairs of different and symbolically significant colors on a purple center, an expression of the *coniunctio oppositorum*.

45
164 × 350 cm
In this kilim the hexagonal figures radiate the same pattern, starting from the central nucleus that contains a double image.

46
79 × 384 cm
The theme of seven recurs in this kilim, in a series of symmetrical figures that seem to outline the shape of a steatopygous goddess. At the sides of these seven images it may be possible to make out white forms representing feline figures.

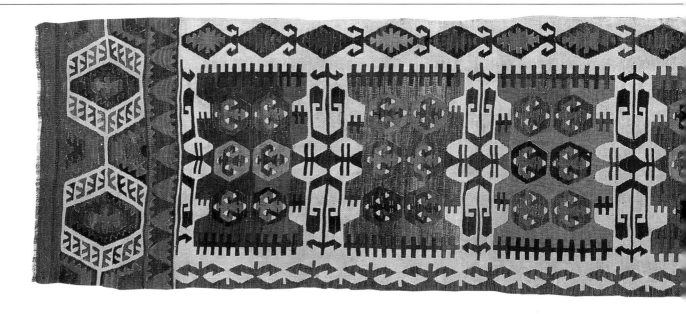

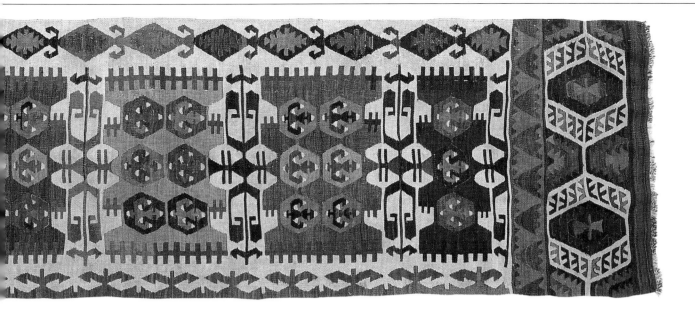

47
188 × 395 cm
The central white area
of the kilim is studded
with tiny symbols. Among
them we can recognize
single and double crosses,
double-headed axes,
some of them in negative,
and other symbols
connected with the
goddess.

48
127 × 147 cm
The stylized images of twenty-eight goddess's heads with segmented arms run along the vertical sides of the kilim, facing alternatively inward and outward.

49
172 × 270 cm
In this kilim, in which the motif of the double-headed axe predominates, the central hexagon-shaped figures are surrounded by the triple image of the goddess, whose legs spread to form two sides of each hexagon.

50
64 × 250 cm
This kilim is divided into seven large mirror images, in which the white geometrical figures represent the Great Goddess. In three of them (the first, fourth and seventh from the right), moreover, the headless goddess grips two double-headed axes.

51
70 × 388 cm
The white hands of the nine headless and symmetrical goddesses hold various attributes of their sovereignty.

52
143 × 322 cm
Looking at this kilim horizontally, we see the head and three-fingered hands of the goddess repeated symmetrically along all four borders.

53
130 × 185 cm
Of the seven "strips" that make up this kilim, three represent stars of Hacilar and four contain hypertrophic images.

54
146 × 280 cm
In this kilim we can see
how the images of the
goddess's heads and
hands, represented
symmetrically, conceal the
double-headed axe in
negative at their center.

55
155 × 258 cm
The symbology of this
kilim, which represents
the ambivalent nature of
the Mother Goddess, is
examined on page 33.

56
132 × 310 cm
In the third and the tenth
hexagon, woven in the
central part of the kilim,
we find two tiny figures
that represent a segment

and a double-headed axe
respectively. Symbolically,
they seem to have the
same meaning of
separation and union at
one and the same time.

57
155 × 290 cm
Purple, the color
representing the union
of opposites, at once
divides and unites, along
an imaginary diagonal, the
symbolic values of this
kilim: chromatic,
numerical and
iconographic.

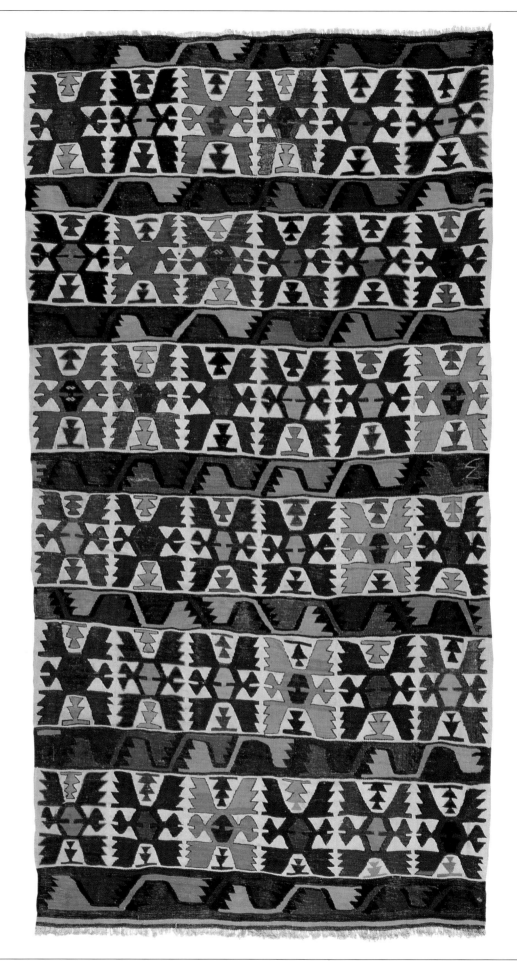

58
154 × 252 cm
The double-headed axe
or its negative inside each
of the six hexagons leads,
in this kilim, to a
hypertrophic
development. In the other
bands, apart from the
central one, the double-
headed axe alternates
with the two-faced head
of the goddess.

59
166 × 264 cm
From the central column of this kilim fourteen double horns branch out in opposite directions. From the two side columns, on the other hand, seven double horns branch off toward the interior of the design.

60
146 × 380 cm
The main characteristic
of this kilim is the double
chromatic sequence of
three colors divided by
a central strip of white,
an expression of spiritual
energy.

61
133 × 230 cm
The stars of Hacilar
depicted in this kilim
contain the symbol of yin
and yang at their center.

62

170 × 330 cm

The figures in the shape of the ace of spades do not obscure the image of the double vulture with bowed head, serrated feathers and feet. However it is shown to be subject to the power of the goddess, here represented in the form of a cross.

63

174 × 430 cm

The stars of David in this kilim bear the symbol of yin and yang at their center. Only the stars on the median line that splits the kilim into two parts are monochromatic and empty in the middle: there was in fact no need to emphasize unity in duality along the line that is in itself an indication of the unity and duality of the whole kilim.

64
162 × 325 cm
The six hands with three
fingers that emerge from
the three rhomboid
figures seem to be
clasping the starry and
purple sky of this kilim.

65
165 × 331 cm
Looking at the kilim
horizontally it is possible
to see, within the eleven
"bands" into which the
rug is divided, vertical
rows of small bull's horns,
some of them containing
designs resembling tuning
forks.

66
185 × 500 cm
The four segmented
figures terminate, on the
outside and inside, in
seven three-fingered
hands.

67
165 × 360 cm
The ten "caves" in
symmetrical pairs give rise
to five geometric figures
that are repeated
concentrically.

68
80 × 222 cm
In this kilim different dual symbols arise inside the twenty-eight rhombuses that make up each of the seven vertical bands.

69
95 × 344 cm
Here the dominant theme is the repetition of a hundred and eleven crosses, enclosed in a variety of ways in its fifteen sections.

70
200 × 334 cm
Looked at horizontally,
we can see, in each of
the four rhombuses, the
symmetrical figures of
six goddesses, with
hyperanthropic arms
in a vertical direction.

71
170 × 335 cm
Twenty-seven, a symbolically significant number in that it is the product of three and nine, is present in this kilim in two different contexts: in the nine horizontal "bands," each containing three rhombuses, and in the three vertical columns, each of which contains nine groups of three rhombuses.

72
186 × 354 cm
Looking at this kilim
horizontally, we can see
how the hands of the
goddess at the ends of the
red and blue fields are
holding pairs of double-
headed axes.

73
138 × 370 cm
The dominant theme, in this case, is provided by the innumerable crosses scattered all over the kilim, and by the symbolic as well as formal relationship that links them to the double rhomboid "caves."

74
180 × 336 cm
The symbolism of the theme of one hundred, the number of white hexagons, is entrusted to a base with a chromatic sequence in which the central band of purple shades off, towards the ends of the kilim, into green, red and blue.

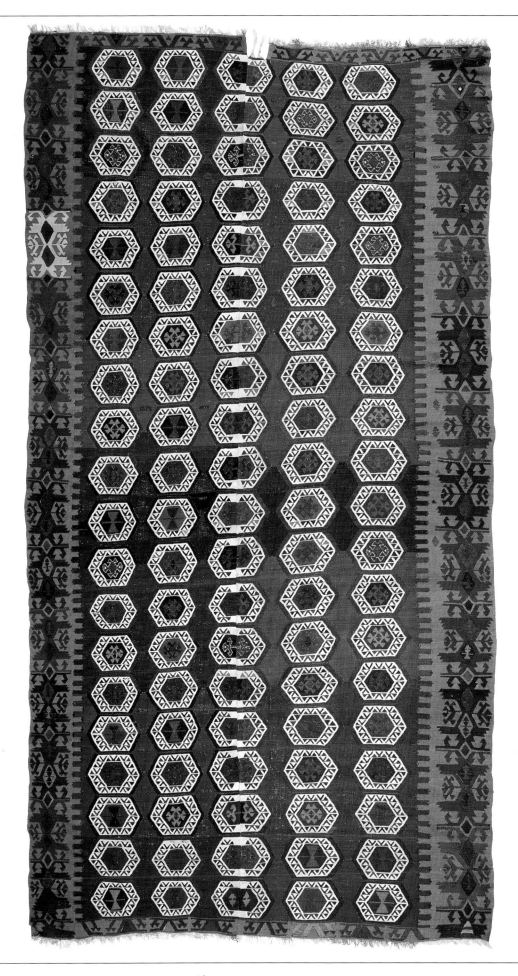

75
158 × 365 cm
In each of the fifty figures
represented on the four
borders of this kilim, it is
possible to make out the
image of three stylized
heads that are reflected
mirrorwise.

76
180 × 400 cm
The white and green
parts of this kilim seem to
derive from the
convergence of two red
and two blue figures. The
association of white with
green creates an intensely
symbolic chromatic unity.

77

182 × 454 cm

Looking at the kilim horizontally we see, in each of the three "bands," twenty-eight female figures with their hands raised to enclose the stylized head made up of three segments.

78
164 × 404 cm
At their point of
convergence, the eighty
stylized images of the
goddess, one mirroring
the other, conceal a
double-headed axe.

79
170 × 305 cm
Between the negatives
and positives of this kilim,
the hands seem to spread
out to emphasize the
symbolism that underlies
them.

80

165 × 280 cm

Looking at the upper and lower borders horizontally, we can see a long and undulating row of double-headed axes. In the central field, on the other hand, we find ten symmetrically opposed figures. In particular, in the central and upper part of the kilim, it is possible to discern the headless body of the goddess with her legs spread and converging on her hands. This convergence creates a cavity in which lie two vultures facing one another.

81
120 × 180 cm
In the ascending sequence of this kilim we can find seven double-headed axes, one of which is set at the top of the vault.

82

161 × 300 cm

Looking at the kilim horizontally, we can see how the figure at top right represents the double mirror image of the headless goddess in red, with the legs spread and converging on the hands. It can also be seen that the cavity produced by this convergence, colored purple on the left, assumes a shape that could be said to resemble a feline lying down, while on the right it outlines a similar shape in negative that can only be guessed at.

83
160 × 265 cm
The symbolic design
of yin and yang is set at
the center of each of the
stars of Hacilar that run
around the edges of this
kilim.

84
158 × 395 cm
At the base of the two opposing and symmetrical images can be found four segments, resembling arms. In one case these are closed in a concave shape, while in the other they open outward. They seem to be related to the central figure, whose ends seem either to be received or rejected by these arms.

85

146 × 500 cm

On the vertical borders of this kilim the double three-fingered hands interlace to form a meandering shape. Along the horizontal borders runs a winding line that emphasizes the stylized head of the goddess, facing alternately inward and outward.

86
145 × 365 cm
Water flows in a triple, closed blue wave. The lake that results from this contains three triple mirror images, similar to the four goddesses on the red ground that surrounds them and from which they seem to have been derived.

87
114 × 440 cm
Water ebbs and flows,
in waves, from the vital
center of the fourteen

symmetrically opposed
goddesses. A more
detailed examination
of this kilim can be found
on page 32.

88
160 × 463 cm
In the twenty-eight figures contained in the seven "bands" of this kilim appears the symmetrically opposed image of the two goddesses gripping the neck of the double vulture, with its feathers in positive and head in negative.

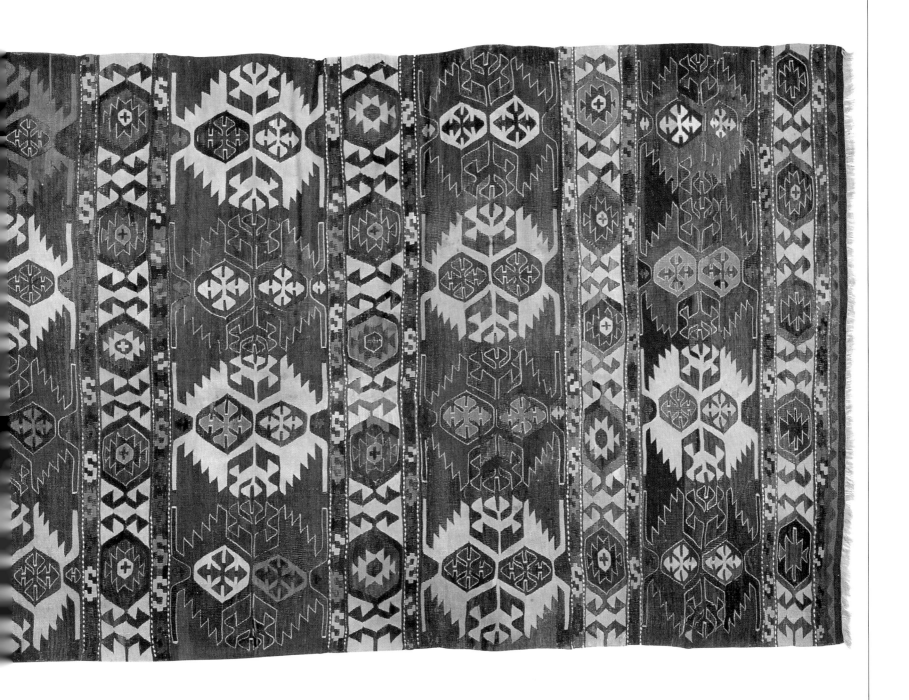

89
82 × 110 cm
The composition of this kilim seems to be telling us that the unity of the rhombus arises from the symmetrical opposition of the double triangle.

90
140 × 230 cm
The central band of this kilim contains four rhombuses indented at the ends to form seventy-two "fingers." Each of the rhombuses encloses the stylized image of a double three-fingered hand.

146

91
196 × 230 cm
Looked at horizontally, the red and blue figures alternate, in the "strips" of this kilim, with the mirror images of the caves, also in red and blue, creating a chromatic contrast.

92
143 × 219 cm
Forty-four red and blue stars of Hacilar float on a black and white ground.

147

93
125 × 183 cm
In the niche of this kilim we can see ten stylized blue hands on a red ground rising toward a triangular vault. The two triple forms on the blue ground could in fact be three, if we consider the niche to be the third constituent element of the white form in the middle.

94
118 × 174 cm
In the six "bands" of this kilim we see pairs of vultures facing one another. At the point where they meet stands the body of the goddess, dominating the power that they represent.

95
67 × 240 cm
The field of this kilim is dominated by the images of ten goddesses set opposite one another with their hands raised.

96
94 × 140 cm
The two converging segments that arise from the two triangles seem to indicate how the way of absorption leads from

small and indecipherable symbols to equally vague and evanescent images.

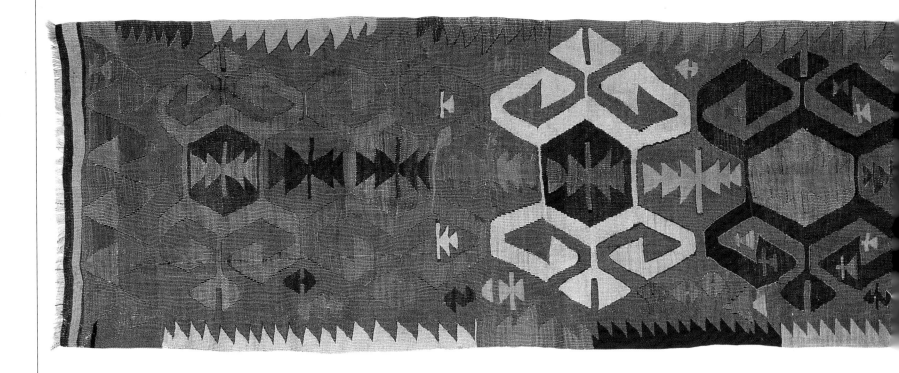

97
81 × 117 cm
The image of the double-headed axe stands at the center of the kilim. At the sides of the rhombus that encloses it can be seen four forms that also contain the image of the double-headed axe, but in negative.

98
83 × 110 cm
This kilim, in which the symbolism of the Mother Goddess dominates, contains repeated images of her power.

99
144 × 382 cm
The concentric rhombuses of this composition seem to arise out of the central nucleus, formed by the double-headed axe, in an emphasis of its original design. At the geometric center of the kilim, the rhombuses meet and form a tiny double triangle, the negative image of the double-headed axe.

100
160 × 391 cm
The fifteen horizontal "bands" in each of the two parts of this kilim are separated by other, narrower "bands" in which tuning-fork patterns alternate with cruciform ones.

101
154 × 380 cm
In this kilim the two rhombuses in the rug reproduced in cat. 99 become three and grow more complicated, developing the symbolism of this number.

155

102
158 × 415 cm
In the middle section of
this kilim, four notched
stars of Hacilar take on
hypertrophic forms,
extending into the brown
of the background.

103
73 × 400 cm
The small symmetrical figures with raised hands that run along three sides of this half of a kilim are similar to the larger ones woven in the central part.

104
140 × 385 cm
This kilim "of the goddess
of rhombuses" is
examined analytically
on page 46.

105
167 × 370 cm
The image of the black

and white goddess
emerges from the central
figure of the kilim.

106
170 × 476 cm
The two orange "bands" in the middle represent the synthesis of an energy that is symbolically expressed by the way the bands change color as they move in toward the center, from blue to red, green and black.

107
170 × 350 cm
In the three segmented
bands of this kilim a triple
and symmetrical

threadlike form emerges
and extends vertically to
link together the spaces
with their different forms
and colors.

108
179 × 437 cm
The four main "bands"
of this kilim are related
to one another in pairs.

This can happen because
the white pattern in one
band is not in the same
position in the next and
vice versa.

109
186 × 283 cm
In this kilim we can see
the recurrent themes of
the arms and the bull's
horns, in positive and
in negative, vertically,
horizontally and opposite
one another.

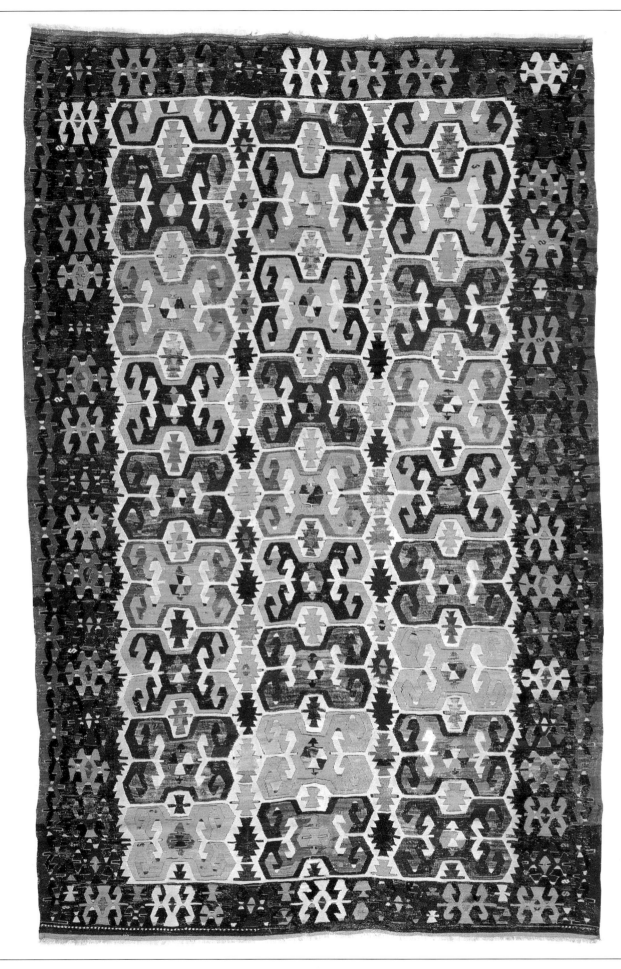

110
156 × 290 cm
The six minor "bands" of
this rug are dominated
by meandering symbols.

111
166 × 440 cm
The slender bodies of the goddesses rise, in some cases with a small head, from the vertices of the seven hexagons and are flanked by other, similar images.

112
166 × 398 cm
The three triple headless goddesses in each of the two parts of the kilim seem to express their sovereignty over the symbolic images of the "cave."

113
160 × 263 cm
The sequence of colors in the seven central figures, mirrored by seven identical ones, is the same as in the niches with seven segments on the upper and lower border of this kilim.

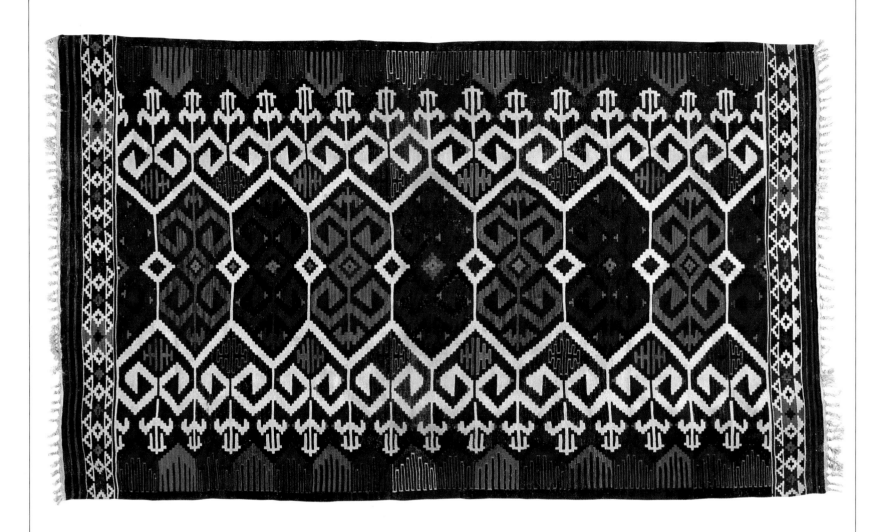

114
116 × 210 cm
Even the small stars of
David appear to have
arms, sprouting from the
ends of each figure in
negative and in positive.

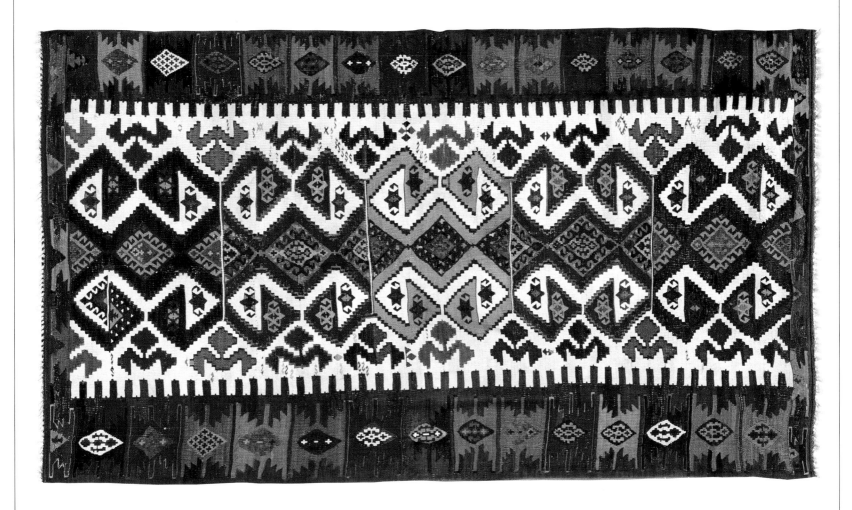

115
79 × 275 cm
In this "kilim of the seven white goddesses" the female figures stand out strongly, invading the whole of the space as if to indicate the immense archetypal force of the maternal energy.

116
137 × 333 cm
The seven mirror images
of the goddess are
surrounded by a white
line that is not broken
anywhere in the kilim.

117
171 × 393 cm
The three central nuclei
that determine the
composition of this kilim
are set inside three
notched stars of Hacilar
and form three rhomboid
figures with nine fingers
per side. Three by nine
is a constant in the
symbolism of this type
of kilim.

118
167 × 362 cm
The hypertrophism
of the figures with "fingers"
spreads out to form
further, symbolically
significant, numerical
correspondences.

119
136 × 210 cm
Examining the interior
of the eight rhombuses
horizontally, the female
figure on a white ground
remains symmetrical. The
vault of the caves above
and below is studded with
stalagmites.

179

120
172 × 260 cm
Among the various symbols that run across the red ground of this kilim we can find four small hexagons with dots, made up of six triangles, three of them black and three white, superimposed in such a way as to conceal the pattern of the star of Hacilar.

121
159 × 275 cm
The dominant symbol
in this kilim is the
double-headed axe, one
of the Mother Goddess's
chief attributes.

122
152 × 240 cm
There are twenty-eight double-headed axes, two in the rhomboid figures and twenty-six on the upper and lower border of the kilim.

123
160 × 250 cm
Looking at this kilim horizontally, it is possible to see the image of two double caves symmetrically opposite one another.

124
77 × 337 cm
The kilim "of the two red
goddesses."

125
93 × 136 cm
The small triangular shape in the middle of the upper border of this kilim indicates that it was intended for use as a prayer rug. The significance of its religious symbolism extends to the colors of the images in the central field.

126
97 × 138 cm
Examined horizontally, we note four large "legs," with four identical ones symmetrically opposite them, in the central field of this kilim.

127
87 × 367 cm
In the lower part of this half kilim we can see nine caves that, connected to their mirror images in the other half, would have formed nine hexagons.

128
134 × 372 cm
At the left-hand end of the white ground a small orange cross set in a purple hexagon appears at the top and the bottom. Other small crosses run along the kilim, with a total of forty in each of the two parts.

129
132 × 256 cm
Looked at horizontally,
the sinuous arms of the
goddess appear on the
white perimeter of each
hexagon, descending
from her head towards
the edges and winding
round the sides of the
hexagon.

130
76 × 276 cm
Mirror images of
arms and horns create
twenty-eight rhombuses.

131
143 × 270 cm
The four rectangles with
a blue and purple ground
contain eighty *wrench-
shaped*, two-faced heads
of the goddess. Between
each of them the
double-headed axe appears in
negative.

132
165 × 260 cm
Looking at the kilim
horizontally we can see,
at the vertex of each
rhombus, the mirror
image of the goddess with
legs spread and
converging on the hands.
The cavity produced by
this convergence is white
like the rest of the kilim,
blending into it to form
new symbols.

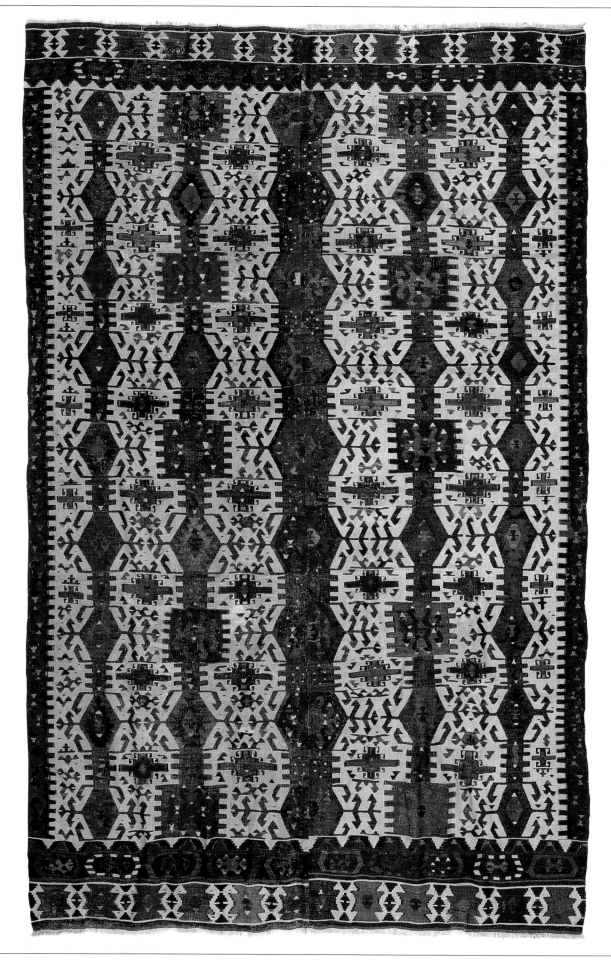

133
184 × 322 cm
Examined horizontally, the two rows of double-headed axes in the middle split the central field of the kilim in half. If we imagine superimposing the two "double-cave" figures on the left side and the two similar figures on the right, we end up with two identical forms.

134
114 × 272 cm
The "kilim of the seven
goddesses": a detailed
examination of this
rug, with its seven
double images of the
deity, can be found on
page 48.

135
94 × 350 cm
The "kilim of time": the six goddesses hold double-headed axes, with half of each depicted in negative and half in positive. They are symbols of the past and future, of calm and storm, since they are symbols of the unity of opposites, a characteristic of matriarchal sovereignty.

136
160 × 260 cm
The four white mirror images and the three that stand out from the blue ground call to mind a stylization of the large horned goddesses of the Middle-Eastern tradition.

137
180 × 360 cm
The difference in size
of the three hexagons
is canceled out by
perspective when the
kilim is observed on the
ground from the distance
of a few paces away from
the smallest hexagon.
Such optical illusions are
not infrequent in kilims.

138
182 × 275 cm
This kilim, originally made up of four central figures, now has only three left. Looking at it horizontally, and observing the pattern of hooked white segments above each figure, we can see the bodies of the headless goddess emerge underneath.

139
65 × 278 cm
The double-headed axe inside each of the three central figures creates the impression of an upward and downward movement from which arise the three double caves.

140
66 × 290 cm
In each of the eighteen serrated quadrilaterals that make up the kilim, a small, white double-headed axe is formed, in negative, at the point where the two opposing heads of the goddess meet.

141
80 × 356 cm
The arms of the goddess or the bull's horns appear in negative or in positive.

142
165 × 360 cm
The unity of this kilim
derives from the six
central figures that seem
intended to represent it.

143
168 × 330 cm
Sixty images of the
goddess run across the
kilim vertically and
horizontally, creating
other forms and images in
negative. The five
notched bands contain
a total of one hundred
other representations
of the goddess.

144
167 × 422 cm
The small white triangles
face one another and link
up on the four borders,

becoming almost
independent of the horns,
in negative or in positive,
to whose ends they are
attached.

145
157 × 455 cm
Six double vultures are
concealed on the white
ground of this kilim

in a stylization of forms
in which, for once, they do
not seem to be subject to
the power of the goddess.

146
164 × 360 cm
Above and below each
row of rhombuses, we see
four rows of seven horns

in negative and in
positive. There are also
twenty-eight small mirror
images at the ends of the
horns.

147
91 × 290 cm
Five slender two-headed
figures separate the five
central hexagons and

seem to link each of the
six upper images to the
corresponding ones
below.

148
84 × 335 cm
If we imagine placing the two white figures at the ends of the kilim alongside one another, we see a double, symmetrically opposed image of the goddess, the same goddess that is repeated, in negative and in positive, twenty-eight times.

149
188 × 360 cm
The seven horizontal
bands are split into the
two halves that constitute
the unity of this kilim.

150
83 × 290 cm
On the upper and lower
border of this kilim we
can see a series of
superimposed and

diverging horns. The
entire surface of the kilim
is dominated by the
presence of S-shaped
hands and double-
headed axes.

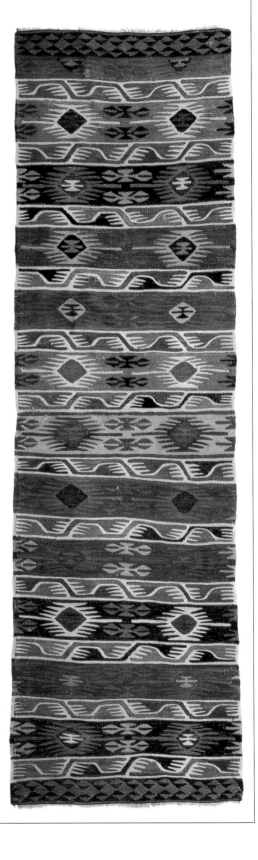

151
175 × 200 cm

In the three main bands of this fragment appear ten small rhomboid figures, each of which contains the double superimposed symbol of the negative of the double-headed axe. From the sides of one of these forms emerge two small arms that make it look like an image of the goddess.

152

152 × 302 cm

At the center of the stars of David with which this kilim is covered appears the symbol of yin and yang. This symbol can also be found inside a row of white rectangles, marked by converging arrowheads, that runs across each band of the central field.

153
180 × 333 cm
Looking at the kilim horizontally, we see forty slender figures on a red ground arise from the stalagmites of the three double caves.

154
109 × 160 cm
The "kilim of the three caves": an analysis of this kilim will be found on page 44.

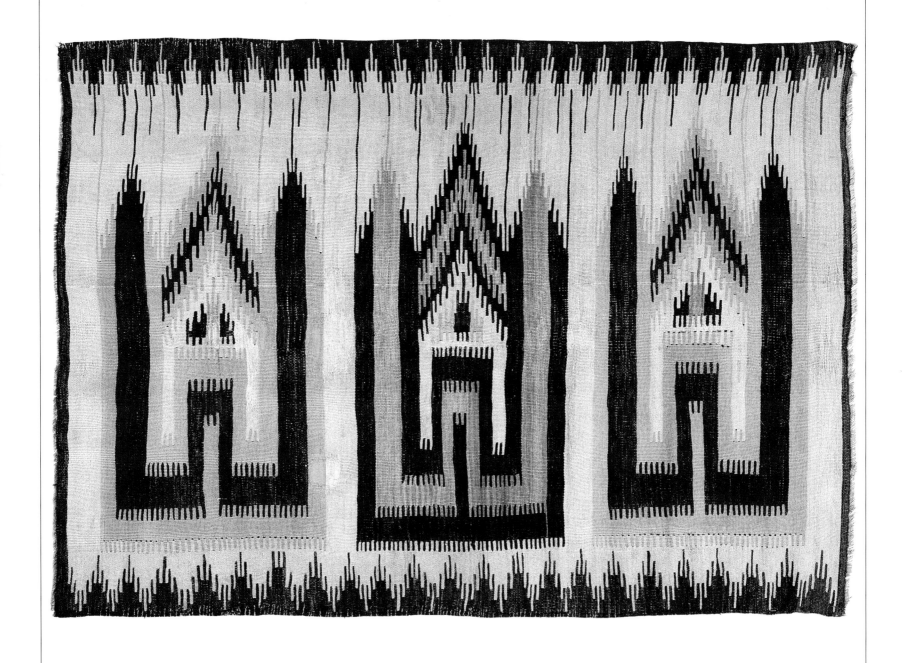

155
160 × 201 cm
The hyperanthropic appearance of the goddess, who has been turned into a mountain, dominates the central field of this kilim, demonstrating the sovereignty of the Great Mother over the earth and the cycle of nature.

References for Illustrations

The illustrations in figs. 2, 3*c*, 4, 5, 6*f*, 7, 9, 14, 15, 16*b*, 21, 22, 30, 31, 34, 45 and 47 (photographs by Arlette Mellaart and Udo Hirsch, drawings by Feridun Oral) are taken from *The Goddess from Anatolia*, vols. I, II and III, Eskenazi, Milan 1989, copyright Udo Hirsch, Adenau, Germany.

The illustration in fig. 12 is taken from J. Makkay, "Neuere Typen der Körös-Starčevo Plastik," in *Journal of Mediterranean Archaeology*, 3, 1985.

The illustration in fig. 13 (drawing by Elena Bachis) is taken from A. Marshack, *The Roots of Civilization: The Cognitive Beginnings of Man's First Art, Symbol and Notations*, McGraw-Hill, New York 1972.

The illustration in fig. 24 is taken from J. Mellaart, "Excavations at Çatal Hüyük: Second Preliminary Report," in *Anatolian Studies*, 1963.

The illustration in fig. 27 (drawing by Patricia Reis) is taken from J. Clottes, M. Carrière, "La statue feminine de Capdenac-le-Haut," in *Congrès Préhistorique de France, 20ième session*, 1974.

The illustration in fig. 28 (photograph by M. Djordievič) is taken from M. Gimbutas, *The Language of the Goddess*, Thames and Hudson, London 1989 and reproduced by kind permission of the National Museum in Belgrade.

The illustration in fig. 29 is taken from S. Alexiou, N. Plato, H. Guanella, *Ancient Crete*, Thames and Hudson, London 1968.

The illustrations in figs. 20 (photograph by Simion/Ricciarini, Milan), 32 (photograph by Giorgio Gualandi, Bologna) are taken from *Archeologia*, Mondadori, Milan 1978. The drawings in figs. 1, 3*ab*, 6*abcde*, 10*abc*, 11*ab*, 16*a*, 18*ab*, 25*ab*, 43*a* and 44*abc* were made by Paolo Pellegrini.

The kilims from Dario Valcarenghi's private collection were photographed by Fabio Davino.